Praise for *The Outdoor Room* and Jamie Durie

'*The Outdoor Room* is bursting with brilliance and imagination ... an innovative and refreshing book jam-packed with ideas and inspiration.'
MELBOURNE WEEKLY

'Durie is clearly an exceptional talent, innovative and passionate about his subject.'
CANADIAN LIVING

'This is an elegant yet practical book, a sumptuous coffee table book, but also a book to draw inspiration from, a book to have you thinking about making more out of your home and garden.'
NOOSA NEWS

'Contemporary photographs in the book are as good-looking as the up-to-the-minute author...'
CANBERRA TIMES

'*The Outdoor Room* emphasises both the practical and the beautiful...'
BURKE'S BACKYARD MAGAZINE

'An inspiring book for anyone wanting to create a ... garden that will blur the boundaries between indoor and outdoor.'
HERALD SUN

'The idea of creating outdoor living spaces is nothing new, but garden designer Jamie Durie puts a fresh look on the concept...'
CONNECTICUT POST

'[*The Outdoor Room*] is your own backyard blitz on a bookshelf.'
BELLE

'*The Outdoor Room* is simply a stunning book, and Jamie's enthusiasm for creativity in the garden is infectious.'
SUNSHINE COAST DAILY

'We can't help but wonder: does Durie make house calls?'
PUBLISHERS WEEKLY

JAMIE DURIE
THE OUTDOOR ROOM

PHOTOGRAPHY BY SIMON KENNY

A SUE HINES BOOK
ALLEN & UNWIN

For architect Geoffrey Bawa, 1919–2003, who has been a constant source of inspiration to me.

A Sue Hines Book
Allen & Unwin
83 Alexander Street
Crows Nest NSW 2065
Australia
Phone: (61 2) 8425 0100
Fax: (61 2) 9906 2218
Email: info@allenandunwin.com
Web: www.allenandunwin.com

National Library of Australia
Cataloguing-in-Publication entry:

Durie, Jamie.
The outdoor room.

1st paperback ed.
ISBN 978 1 74175 021 8.

ISBN 1 74175 021 0.

1. Gardens – Design. 2. Landscape gardening. 3. Landscape design. I. Title.

712.6

The photographs on pages 13–18 are by Donna North and photographs on pages 112–13, 130, 132, 179 are by Harriet Rowe. All sketches and plans are by Patio.

The author and publishers are grateful to Anibou for their loan of the table used in the cover photograph and to the following companies for supplying images: alloy-homewares, House of Bamboo, Eco Concepts, Box & Dice, Fractal Systems (pp30–1); Eco Concepts, Urbanstone, Austimber Supplies, Rock 'n Stone, Fractal Systems (pp66–7); Made from Steel, Industree, House of Bamboo, Motyaj Potteries, Eco Concepts (pp88–9); Spence & Lyda, Bisque Interiors, Barlow Casual Furniture, alloy-homewares, Kezu (pp96–7); Clear Solutions Bathware (p135); Light on Landscapes (p199).

Designed and typeset by MAU Design
Printed in Singapore by Imago

10 9 8 7 6 5 4 3 2 1

CONTENTS

INTRODUCTION WELCOME TO THE
OUTDOOR ROOM

Since the publication of *Patio*, I've been swamped with requests for more detailed information about how to achieve the distinctive look of the Patio designs featured in the book. Well, I could go on for several volumes about the technical side of things, but on the conceptual side, it's true to say that every one of my projects is based on simple principles and a combination of instinct and imagination. When the time came to sit down and write a second book, it made sense for me to concentrate on expanding those ideas and to share some of my theories and philosophies as well as a couple of trade secrets along the way.

Why the Outdoor Room? At the risk of sounding like a fanatic, I'm a firm believer that outdoor living spaces in our homes should be a whole lot more than just another place to carry out domestic activities. They have the potential to play a crucial role in nurturing personal wellbeing and in helping us to find both inner and outer peace in our daily lives. Exposure to fresh air, water, plants and sunshine immediately reconnects us to our essential humanity. When we live in the city – and most of us do – we can't climb a mountain, walk along a beach or wander through a forest every day, but we can endeavour to bring evocative symbols of these things into our homes.

No matter how large or small your exterior space, there's something in here for you. A big empty expanse is probably the hardest to start with because there are no boundaries, but step by step you can break it down into smaller, more intimate compartments for a series of fully livable locations. By the same token, don't think you need a minimum area to work with; even a small balcony can include all the basic elements of life. This then, is my definition of an outdoor room.

The following chapters cover what I believe to be the seven fundamental components of a beautiful and functional space. I haven't set out to write a technical manual – my aim is to provide inspiration balanced with a range of practical ideas and solutions. You'll see more detailed information here than in *Patio*, more hints and tips for you to apply. There are style guide pages, packed with products and materials that I use every day, and, of course, photographs speak for themselves so there's an abundance of gorgeous outdoor rooms to spark your imagination.

I've tried whenever I can to include suggestions to help you picture the results before you take the plunge. Using these visual aids is a good safety precaution but, more than that, it's a whole lot of fun to mess around building walls and stages out of boxes and broomsticks and sheets. Play is such an important part of the creative process, so forget about who's watching, just go for it and enjoy!

On a more sober note, in this era of global warming we can no longer ignore the devastating repercussions of human activity on this world of ours. The tremendous need for us all to work towards saving what's left of our beautiful planet is a major preoccupation of mine. You can see how this issue heavily influences my choice of plants, as most of them are hardy, robust and drought-resistant. You'll also see an emphasis on using sustainable organic materials like plantation timbers and bamboo and, wherever possible, choosing recycled or re-used commodities. Last but definitely not least, every chapter contains a special 'eco-tip' to help you make choices that will be less damaging to the environment and work towards ensuring a better future for our children.

I've loved making this book. The process of putting it together has forced me to reflect on some important life decisions and really clarify my design philosophy. It's also filled me with a new rush of enthusiasm for the enormous potential of our outdoor living spaces and the peace and pleasure they can bring us.

My hope is it will inspire you, too.

CHAPTER ONE THE WALLS

DEFINING THE SPACE

Recently I was talking through ideas for this book with some friends, and was amazed at how many of them assumed that I always start with the floor when I begin a design. My reply was simply, 'You wouldn't put carpet down in an indoor room if there weren't any walls yet, so why would you lay a floor in an outdoor room if the area wasn't yet defined?' Whether walls are soft form (plant, screen) or hard form (stone, timber), they are ultimately what outlines the space so establishing where to position them and what kind of material they'll consist of can make or break the feel and the functionality of your outdoor room.

First and foremost, walls create intimacy and security. Remember what it felt like when you first spent the night in a tent? Only a thin slice of fabric between you and the elements but the sense of enclosure made you feel cosy and protected. The simple fact is that the larger the space the more it lacks the intimacy that characterises the outdoor room. A big country garden might be a daunting prospect to begin with, but you'd be amazed how you can instantly overcome this empty feeling by breaking it up into smaller compartments with solid or temporary partitions or by experimenting with levels.

Aesthetically, dressing the walls is a great opportunity to establish the personality of your outdoor room, providing a vertical canvas where you can express whatever you desire. Because of my theatrical background, I can't help thinking of this process as being like the process of dressing a stage: the screens are the wings, the levels are the platforms and the boundary walls are the rear curtains or backdrops. Then I work in the accent plants to act like props, the groundcovers to serve as smoke, dry ice or mist ... you get the picture!

COR-TEN IS EASILY bent into unusual shapes, so it's the ideal material for this rambling, large-scale serpentine wall. Slicing through the landscape, the sheets overlap like fish scales and stand on their own strength and balance. The principle behind this structure was to create an organic sculptural form using hard geometrical steel with a natural weathered finish. It coils around the plant beds, contrasting starkly with soft, feathery drifts of grass. Horizontal sprays of water surge from between the cor-ten sheets, accentuating the dramatic movement of the curve. Behind the S-shaped curve is a blade wall made of sheets of cor-ten metal (overleaf), with rows of delicate silver-birch saplings embedded in a valley of soft black mulch between the blades. The surface of the cor-ten will rust over time, taking on the rich ochre hue seen here, but will not corrode to the point of decay.

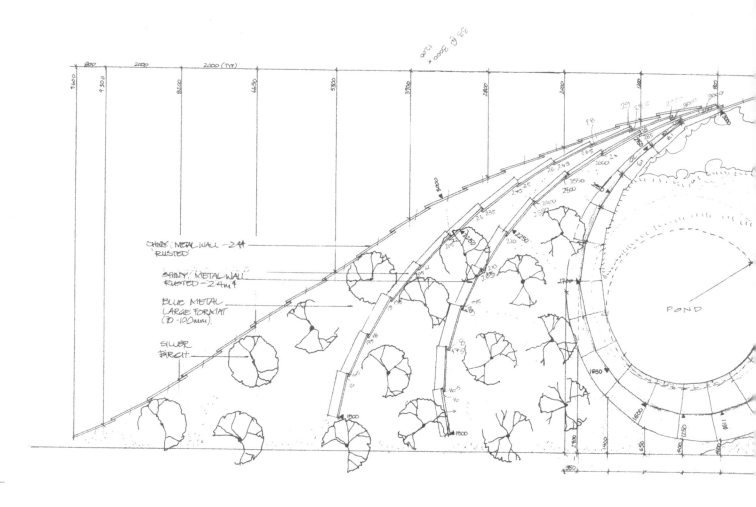

SHINY METAL WALL – 2.4+
RUSTED

SHINY METAL WALL
RUSTED – 2.4m +

BLUE METAL
LARGE FORMAT
(70-100mm).

SILVER
BIRCH.

POND

SCALE   1:50

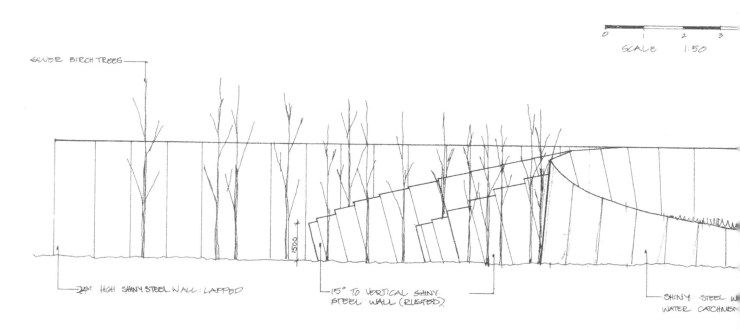

SILVER BIRCH TREES

2.4M HIGH SHINY STEEL WALL: LAPPED

15° TO VERTICAL SHINY.
STEEL WALL (RUSTED)

SHINY. STEEL W.
WATER CATCHMEN

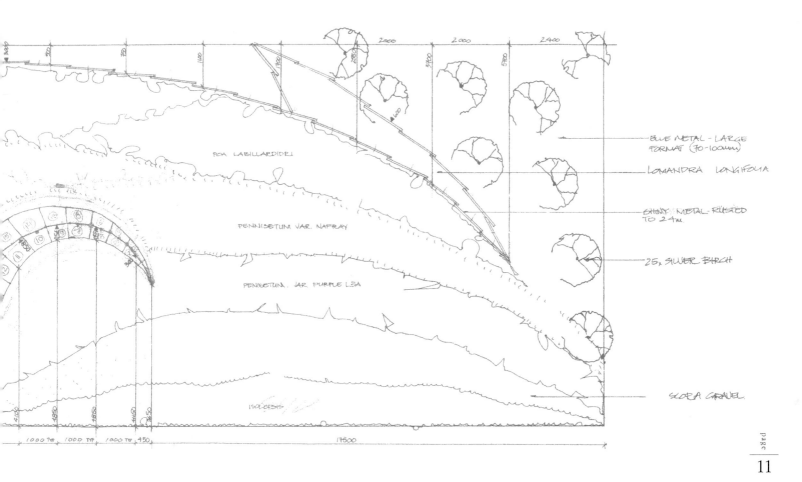

POA LABILLARDIERI

PENNISETUM VAR. NAFRAY

PENNISETUM. VAR. PURPLE LEA

ISOLEPSIS

BLUE METAL - LARGE FORMAT (70-100mm)

LOMANDRA LONGIFOLIA

SHINY METAL - RUSTED TO 2.4m

25 x SILVER BIRCH

SCORIA GRAVEL

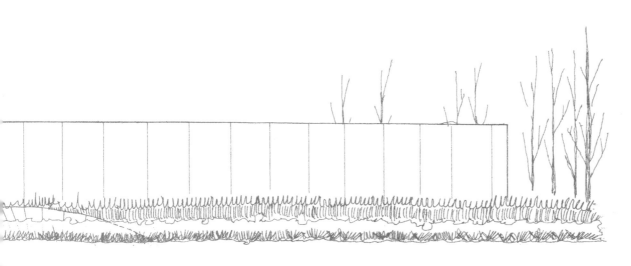

PLANT SCHEDULE

BOTANICAL NAME	COMMON NAME	SIZE	QTY.
Betula pendula	Silver Birch	3m	25
Isolepis nodosa	Knobby Club Rush	8"	
Lomandra longifolia	Spiny Headed Mat Rush	8"	
Pennisetum alopecuroides 'Nafray	Swamp Foxtail Grass	8"	
Pennisetum alopecuroides 'Purple Lea'	Swamp Foxtail Grass	8"	
Phalaris arundinacea var. picta	Variegated Reedy Grass	8"	
Poa labillardiera	Poa	8"	

PROS AND CONS

Even before you start, make sure you're clear about how the room is going to be used. Will it be primarily a private refuge for contemplation and relaxation or will it need lots of seating options and open areas for entertaining the hordes? Then go out and have a good hard look at the space and identify what I call all the 'liabilities' and the 'assets'. For example, a liability could be a neighbour's window close to your property, a nearby highway or other intrusive traffic noise, a pedestrian path immediately outside or a backyard that overlooks yours. All these are potential trespassers infringing on your privacy, and they need to be screened or muffled as efficiently as possible.

One of your greatest assets could be an attractive view, however small. A bush or ocean outlook, a shady tree arching over a neighbour's fence, a glimpse of a city skyline – these fall under the category of assets. An indoor room that opens directly onto the outdoor room is also a huge advantage, especially if it's an entertainment area. Whatever you do, don't block access by placing things like planters between; keep the segue smooth with the lines flowing and you instantly blend two opposing spaces into one very versatile and interesting whole.

Now that you've decided where you want the walls to be, get out the old pencil and paper and draw some pictures. Don't hold back if you're not much of an artist: I'm a shocking scribbler myself but it's a great way of getting your ideas out of your head and onto paper so that you can start manipulating them into working dimensions. The next step might get you some strange looks but it's a brilliant way to test your ideas in situ. Grab a couple of broomsticks, string a rope between them and hang a sheet over the top to emulate where the potential wall would be. Leave it there for a day and you may discover a wall would block out vital sunlight at the most important time of the morning or afternoon. To be honest, this is also where you're going to have the most fun. Playing around with simple visual aids like this can get you really excited about what could be and shows you how to make the most of what's yours.

FINAL FRONTIER

Security is a must these days, especially in built-up areas. We've all got valuable possessions to protect, but most of all, we need to feel our families are safe from intruders. A solid wall is the decisive barrier for privacy and protection so, where budget permits, solid brick or stone is the strongest and most enduring option to go for. Otherwise, any wall over 1.8 metres tall constructed of a material that offers no possibility of a foothold can be considered secure.

THE THEME OF this garden, featured in the Ellerslie Flower Show in Auckland, New Zealand, is Australian landscape. A river divides the 'dry' side, representing the desert, and the 'wet' side, representing the rainforest. The spectacular cane sculptures rising from the water were directly inspired by the idea of Aboriginal fishing baskets, and the stepping-stones curled around them are reminiscent of swirling Aboriginal dot paintings.

THE ELLERSLIE SHOW is a wonderful opportunity for experimentation, and this one has some particularly innovative feature walls. Seen here are some super-sturdy barriers where panels of reinforcing mesh are attached to upright timber sleepers to form mini-cages. Filled with 50–150mm-diameter river pebbles, they can also be sectioned off horizontally to make windows. Every view was carefully planned for maximum effect.

DRIFTWOOD IS A marvellously evocative material to work with and here (top right) it forms a sculptural end-pillar to a plain rendered wall. Every piece was stacked to fit snuggly within the timber frame, bringing waves of movement and striking texture to a simple, functional boundary.

If you want to disguise the base material, there's a wide selection of finishes available, from tile-cladding to a range of different renders. Bagging is probably one of the easiest finishes to apply. A thin coating of sand and cement mix is sponged on to give a uniform texture while still showing the uneven surface of the bricks or stones beneath. At the other end of the spectrum you have methods like Spanish rendering where a coating of the mix is pasted on in thick random smears, much like spreading a layer of peanut butter on toast. As for the colour finish, there's an enormous palette to choose from so it's up to you whether to highlight it as a feature wall or encourage it to blend in with the surroundings.

Timber is a fantastic permanent wall and can be as sturdy as stone, depending on the way it's constructed. A simple treated-pine timber paling fence is structurally sound, won't rot, and laid butt-to-butt will prevent an intruder from gaining a foot- or hand-hold. Ensure you have a decent-sized cap (at least 45mm x 120mm) at the top and the bottom and you have all the strength you need as well as a nice sturdy look. Best of all, you are using a renewable resource and that's got to be good.

If you need strength, but wish to avoid the 'blockiness' of a solid wall, timber palings can be swivelled on edge to make a vertical shutter. Timbers are placed so they angle

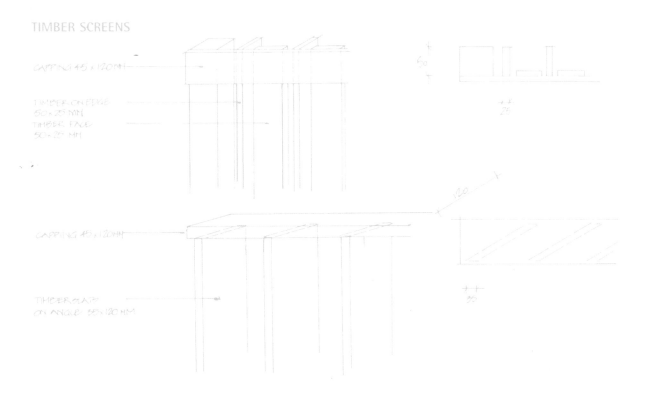

TIMBER SCREENS

THE STANDARD TIMBER paling fence need not be visually dull, as we see here, with every second plank laid on edge (above) and with the timbers fixed on an angle assuring privacy and the continued flow of light and air (below).

towards your biggest liability, screening it from view. Spaced with roughly 75mm between, a series of 25 x 110mm boards will give you plenty of ventilation with enough light to keep the backs of shrubs thriving and less risk of fungal disease on your plants.

Alternatively, you can sink treated pine sleepers about 700mm into the ground in a soldier-course formation (neatly parallel and evenly spaced). Firmly encased in a concrete footing they are an inpenetrable boundary and will need no other form of support. Try experimenting with paint – a different colour for every face – which accentuates the form of the timber. Set some low-voltage lights between the sleepers for a dramatic night-time effect where slim shafts of light shoot off into the darkness.

I love the look of a rippling S-shaped serpentine wall. Its gentle, sinuous curves create niches that present a perfect opportunity to show off interesting plants or features. Best of all, it provides its own structural support requiring only basic footings because each opposing radius offsets the other.

Semi-spaced block-work walls are making a welcome comeback. This is where you construct a lattice-like boundary by leaving gaps between the bricks. The method has long been popular with commercial properties, but it can look fabulous in a domestic environment where the openings created by the missed bricks become ready-made shelves for pots or pieces of art. You can have lots of fun with paint, too. Try one colour on the face and a contrast on the sides so that as you move alongside it a two-tone effect springs out at the viewer. Like the serpentine wall, this one is also very flexible and can turn easily because the bricks are not positioned butt-to-butt.

THE SOMETIMES SCREEN

Semi-permanent partitions and screens are what I call 'temporary' divisions which can provide shade, a gentle border, a sense of privacy and the delightful bonus of atmospheric elements like shadows and dappled light. I tend to favour natural materials for the way they drift in the breeze and diffuse the sunlight.

TIMBER SCREEN

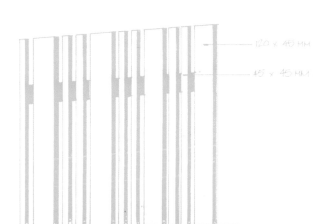

SOLDIER-COURSE SLEEPER SCREEN

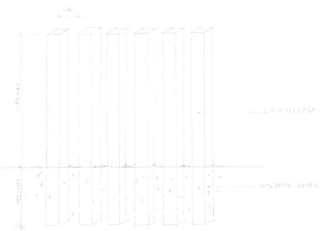

WOVEN ROPE
SCULPTURE

GABION + SLEEPER
RETAINING WALL

WOVEN ROPE SCULPTURE
LIT ON INSIDE
WITH MISTER WITHIN

REFLECTION POND

CREEK BED PLAN
GRAVEL + GRASS

SECTION.

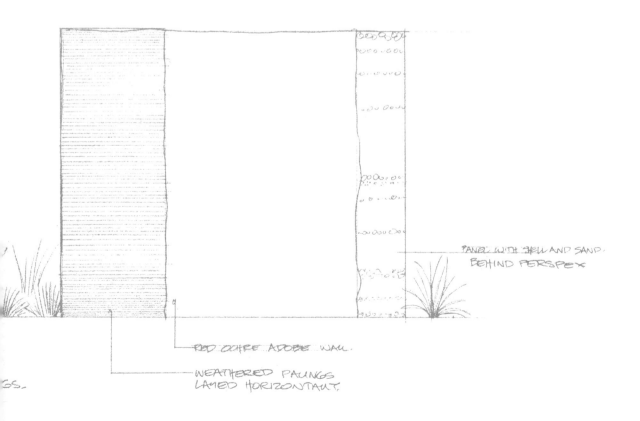

PANEL WITH SHELL AND SAND.
BEHIND PERSPEX

RED OCHRE ADOBE WALL.

WEATHERED PALINGS
LAYED HORIZONTALY.

GS.

Reed blinds (again, I recommend Natureed) make a fine linear partition, and the reeds making up the sheets come in a variety of width measurements from anywhere between 5mm and 75mm. Bamboo screens are excellent light filters and I'm particularly fond of the Japanese versions which are lashed together with rope rather than nailed together so they are entirely organic.

Sails continue to be a popular screen choice, but canvas is rarely used these days as it's had to make way for the more durable plastic. Traditionally used for shading, sails are a wonderful vertical partition and allow you to play with vibrant colours and different shapes. Don't limit yourself with the kinds of materials you choose for screening. As long as

a product can withstand the elements, you can use it anywhere in the space, so think outside the square.

GREEN WALL

Fresh, tactile and fabulous to look at, nothing beats a layered bank of shrubs and perennials, curtains of delicate climbers and perhaps a tree or two towering at the back. I see the transition from groundcover to shrub to tree as part of a single plant zone, so my green wall might constitute an area that extends back as far as two or three metres. But before you dive in and begin planting, make sure the conditions are right. Is there enough sun to encourage a decent spread of tree foliage, for example? Is the soil deep enough, rich enough and well

SURROUNDED BY LESS *dominant plants, this* Echium *(Pride of Madeira, left) is a lush centrepiece to a textural green wall. In summer the mounds of grey-green foliage form a cloudy backdrop to the resplendent spires of its brilliant blue flowers. MASSIVE TERRAZZO PLANTERS outside this busy city shopping complex (centre) hold a self-contained green screen with large drooping fronds of* Strelitzia nicolai *and Fan Palms. A MAGNIFICENT STAND of Stripy Bamboo (*Bambusa multiplex *cv., right), its sturdy, tapering trunks softened by wispy clusters of leaves.*

enough drained to support a variety of root formations? Is the soil sandy or does it have a heavy clay content?

Then comes the choice of plants, and this is where knowledge is the key. Only when you know the potentials and limitations of a variety of species do you have the tools to sculpt your wall successfully. I would recommend you systematically go through the plants available, and the best way to do this is to get your hands on a Botanica. (I never leave home without one!) A good quality plant reference manual will tell you all the basics about what the plant needs to survive and how big it will grow and usually it will provide a picture alongside the plant description so you can visualise how it will look in the space. Once you've studied the plants' survival characteristics, choose those that are appropriate to the shape, colour and texture you desire and the specific conditions of your space.

Another good idea is to go for a walk around your local Botanic Gardens taking note of the magnificent varieties of plants available and checking the labels as you go. When I was studying horticulture I would steal away whenever possible and eat my lunch walking around the Botanic Gardens. I learnt a huge amount from these brief wanders and, I must admit, not a day goes by when I don't miss those peaceful and inspirational lessons.

Keep in mind that different plants develop in different ways so you need to identify which types of growth will suit the purposes of your outdoor room.

HEDGING is the obvious green wall and thankfully, we've come a long way from the generic Box hedge. Lilly pilly makes a wonderful thick boundary, as do *Pittosporum* 'James Stirling', camellias, photinias, murrayas, viburnums and robinias. Some eucalypts work well for a lighter structure, along with *Michelia figo*, NZ flax, *Westringia* spp. and even coprosmas for a beachfront property. Any of the clumping bamboos do a fine job of providing vertical cover while still allowing light to filter through.

ALL THE BEST ideas are right in front of you, and more often than not, they come from nature – note the incredible formation of these branches. This Dracaena draco *lives in Sydney's Botanic Gardens. As you can see, we're very close.*

AERIAL PLEACHING is the method whereby you strip back all the lower branches of the shrub to reveal the trunk and the outstretched branches above join up to form a continuous canopy. Lilly pillies, pittosporums, robinias, pears and citrus work particularly well, but make sure the plants are not so close that they crowd together and bulge. What you're aiming for is a continuous wall of green where the tips of the laterally spreading upper foliage touch to create a solid aerial hedge. A finely pleached hedge looks magnificent up-lit against a wall or if free-standing it can form an arched window channelling the eye towards a garden view beyond. Pleaching also encourages the growth of a lower storey of foliage because the light coming through the naked trunks ensures a level of contrasting shrubbery can thrive below.

CLIMBERS are great for disguising an ugly surface. Twining and scrambling plants work around what's there whereas root climbers make their mark on the surroundings. *Ficus pumila* is one of the most aggressive and adhesive climbers I know with shoots that will eventually work their way into the brickwork. If you trim off the adolescent trunk and woody build-up and keep it all immature growth, the *Ficus* will maintain a tight, compact cover. Keep an eye on this one because it can get away from you and it's hard to get rid of once it's established, but this truly is the ultimate growing wall that will retain its architecture forever.

A SCREEN WALL can be used to draw people in to a garden or to frame a view. Fencing an area will also encourage the viewer to focus on a part of the garden they might not have noticed (left). PAVING COVERS MOST of this substantial suburban outdoor room (right) so treated pine fencing was deliberately chosen to contrast with its hard angular lines. The horizontal timber baton screens are fixed in an alternating double layer so neighbours can't see in, but the void in between allows light and breezes to pass through. A pillar water feature breaks up the lengthy wooden expanse.

the simple things

Garden design is constantly evolving – that's just one of the reasons why I'm hooked. I'm still relatively new to this career, and although I've learnt a great deal in five years, I'm well aware there's so much more to know. You never stop coming across new techniques, absorbing new ideas and, little by little, gaining the confidence to trust your instincts. I'm forever being surprised and challenged by the possibilities presented to me and delighted by the reactions of my clients when the picture in my head translates into a reality before their eyes.

Several months back I designed a series of outdoor rooms for a young businessman and his partner. The property was stunning: lavish and opulent with some breathtaking features. They loved what we did to the place, but funnily enough, their favourite addition ended up being a small, simple outdoor yoga room with clean lines and minimal fittings.

A classic example of that wise and wonderful adage: Less Is More.

Other less aggressive climbers on my list of favourites are Chilean Jasmine (*Mandevilla*), Madagascar Jasmine (*Stephanotis* sp.) and *Hardenbergia* with its pretty purple flower. If you want to cover up an old wall in a hurry, put in a passionfruit vine which will spread swiftly and be laden with fruit in the summer months.

ESPALIER is a rare sight these days, but to me there's nothing more elegant than a fruiting or flowering wall smothered in fragrant blossoms. It's a time-consuming process which involves a fair bit of finicky work whereby all the front and rear branches are pruned back and the lateral branches are trained along a trellis, cable or fence. However, if you do decide to commit time and energy to an espaliered wall, the rewards are great, especially if you choose a shrub that both flowers and fruits, allowing you to observe the seasons changing and enjoy its bounty all year round. Camellias, roses and star jasmine are good options.

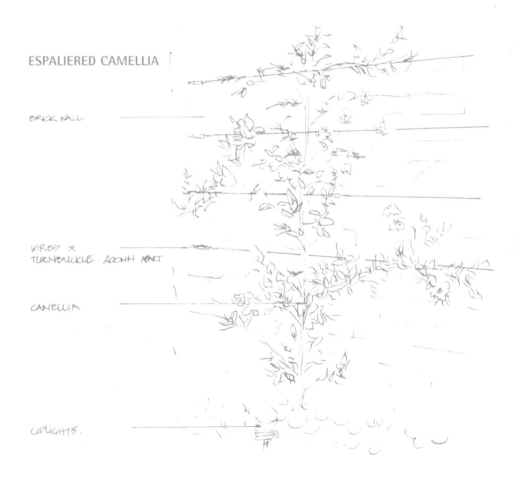

ESPALIERED CAMELLIA

BRICK WALL

WIRES x
TURNBUCKLE 600MM APART

CAMELLIA

UPLIGHTS.

inspiration
WALLS

above and beyond

Complete or partial ceilings aren't a priority in most outdoor rooms, but there are few that wouldn't benefit from a degree of overhead cover. I've had clients who like to do as much living outside as possible – rain, hail or shine – so they need constant protection from the changing elements. You might have a piece of furniture or artwork or some sound equipment that isn't weatherproof. You might have a particularly exposed space and want to incorporate some kind of permanent shield from the harmful effects of the harsh antipodean sun. Then there are the statistics that tell us more and more Australians are choosing to work from home. I can't imagine a more pleasant and energising space to locate part or all of your home office than your outdoor room (but you might need additional shelter to protect computer hardware and so on).

Corrugated plastic products are an extremely cost-effective option. As long as the sheets are fixed on at least a 5-degree angle, water won't build up and stagnate between the layers. Glass and perspex form a clean, clear protective shield, and I recommend some timber slats over the top to provide shade.

PRIME TIME FOR *showing off the alang-alang pavilion is evening. Strategically placed globes project a mellow, honeyed wash, highlighting the tightly wound batons of* Imperata *grass to perfection. Restful and airy by day, the room takes on an extraordinary feeling of warmth and intimacy when plunged into darkness.*

Sailcloths are a great cover but be aware that they are not all waterproof and sunproof. Materials range from 20 per cent UV protection to total blockout so choose the right product for the right situation.

Personally, I like to feel that I'm surrounded with as much organic material as possible so most of my favourite shade structures are made of natural products that allow light and air to filter through. You can disguise the more austere structures by cladding with timber, bamboo, Natureed or branches of tea-tree.

My all-time number one roof structure would have to be the thatched 'alang-alang' pergola from Indonesia. Impervious to moisture, its waterproofing capacity increases with the years because the principal material, the grass *Imperata cylindrica*, packs down and knits together in much the same way as feathers on a duck's back. The interior detail of the alang-alang is stunning. I love gazing up at the neat wads of grass wrapped tightly around bamboo rods in perfect symmetry. And the fragrance of the thatching material is spicy and evocative, instantly transporting me back to my beloved Bali.

HERE WE SEE *how the alang-alang roof was deliberately tilted towards the viewer to emphasise its intricate internal structure. Lush plantings, incremental level changes, a shallow pool embracing the forecourt and a rich purple retaining wall along the back all contribute to a sense of peaceful sanctuary.*

*THAI SILK BOLSTERS (below) supply
flamboyant colour to contrast with tawny timber
and golden thatch, while the detail of the alang-
alang ceiling (below right) is surely a work of art
in itself.*

CHAPTER TWO THE
FLOOR
A BASE ON WHICH TO BUILD

Now that you've shaped your space, it's time for the groundwork to begin. The floor – and by that I mean everything that sits on the ground of the outdoor room – is an intrinsic part of its visual impact, connecting and unifying all the different elements, blending inside and out and being touched in some way by every single person who enters.

Steps, decks or platforms and pathways are a vital structural consideration and must be built around the same time as fixing the walls. However, the material for the floor will often be the last thing you decide on because it will be dictated by things like the prevailing colour theme, the choice of plants, the placement of tables and chairs and the amount of wear and tear it will have to cope with.

The good news is that the technology of floor products has advanced in leaps and bounds. Pavers installed at Homebush for the 2000 Sydney Olympics were a world-famous example of this. A series of modular interlocking pieces riddled with tiny holes that allowed water to run through just like natural soil, they reduce the run-off that pollutes our drainage system and precious oceans. Exciting innovations like these are just the tip of the iceberg when it comes to exterior floor surfaces.

I use stone and pavers a lot because they are so practical for high traffic areas, but wherever appropriate I will install a surface that encourages people to decrease the pace a little. This comes from a Japanese philosophy, to slow down the viewer so they appreciate what's around them more. A good way of achieving this is to build large wooden pontoons in stepping-stone formation (or just put in some stepping stones) and then plant everything in between and around them. Not only do you feel light and elevated (almost a floating sensation), but because the path is broken up, you're gently coerced into taking that little bit of extra care with your steps and consequently a little more time to soak up the surroundings. Obviously, if you've got to wheel your bin or bicycle through there, you'll need to join up the pontoons for easier access, but this is still a fine technique for enhancing the enjoyment of the outdoor room.

LEVEL-HEADED

Once in a blue moon I'll find myself in a big space with a client staring at me in eager anticipation and I'm completely stuck for ideas. Then suddenly I'll picture a series of raised flowerbeds or a sunken dining area and the creative juices instantly start flowing again.

Introducing a change of level, even as small as 250mm, can transform a space, and the

evidence of this is all around us. Nature knows no bounds when it comes to levels: trees and shrubs are random heights and ever-changing; mountains, valleys, cliffs and ravines are all part of a structural template that we can pick up on and bring into our gardens. It may not be so easy to achieve inside our homes, but the outdoors lend themselves to such creativity.

Start with the section where you're going to spend the most time, whether relaxing or entertaining, and work on achieving a 'sunken' feel so that it's more enclosed and intimate.

If there's a section with an outlook, think about raising it to capitalise on the view. (A sunbathing area that looks down on the pool is a fine opportunity to do this.)

DESIGNED AS A busy public thoroughfare, the abundance of this space presented a fabulous opportunity to introduce natural elements into what is traditionally a very corporate environment. Slashing through an ordered promenade of paving is a narrow creek bed fringed with river stones and reeds. Just a glimpse of this trickling waterway makes you want to take off your shoes and socks and go for a refreshing paddle.

MINIATURE STARBURSTS of Pieris *'Red Mill'* *sweep the earth beneath Chinese Elms* (Ulmus parvifolia), *alleviating the hefty bulk of the basalt blocks that make up the retaining wall.*

'JUST LIKE THE COMBINATION OF SOMETHING OLD AND SOMETHING NEW, THE MARRIAGE OF NATURAL FORM AND MAN-MADE INTRODUCES A LOVELY SENSE OF BALANCE.'

A VERITABLE CATALOGUE *of floor options.* *Through the sentry-like timber screen painted to* *complement the autumn colours (left), mounds of* *deep crimson* Loropetalum *'Burgundy' lead to an* Acer palmatum *'Globosum' (Plane Tree) on a bed* *of* Pieris *'Red Mill' interspersed with chalky white* *pebbles for contrast. Stepping-stones traverse the* *slow-moving creek bed (right), banked by river* *stones and reeds and clumps of* Isolepsis nodosa *(Knobby Club Rush) and* Lomandra hystrix *(Matt Rush).*

Elevating plant beds makes caring for your plants easier and highlights the structure and form of the leaves, but do ensure that drainage is adequate to cope with the run-off. And, of course, when you're planning stairs and levels, keep in mind wheelchair and pram access as well as the needs of any elderly friends and family.

Visualising changing levels in the mind's eye is a skill that I hope will never leave me, but for many people, this is not something that comes easily. Fortunately, anyone can trial the look they're going for by building temporary stages out of planks, milk crates, cardboard boxes and anything else that will demonstrate how a change of level will affect the room. It might look a bit like a *Play School* set, but it really works.

Small courtyards rarely need them, but clearly defined pathways are a must in a large garden, guiding the feet and leading the eye to features and destinations. Unless it's a primarily functional space, I prefer a curved, meandering path. Even the more formal, linear gardens benefit from a bending pathway which introduces a subtle visual balance.

A word of warning: don't fall into the trap of getting so carried away that the trail ends up too complex. People will become bored winding back and forth with no apparent reason, so make sure there's a purpose to every twist and turn.

STICKS AND STONES

Probably the biggest decision you'll have to make about the floor is the type of material you'll choose. Much will depend on how the room will be used. Will it have to put up with kids' wear and tear? Will your pets spend a lot of time out there? Or will it be primarily ornamental so the look and feel of it is the top priority? Bear in mind that light colours open up a smaller space, making it look larger. And a hot space in full sun for much of the day will benefit from a lightly tinted floor surface that won't reflect the light or promote a feeling of stuffiness.

PAVERS fit the bill in just about any situation. They're hardy, versatile, cost-effective and come in every colour of the rainbow. Laying them is relatively easy:

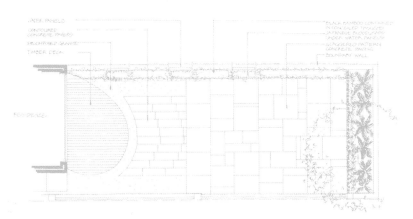

ONE LEVEL MADE up of four distinctly different floor materials makes this small courtyard look much larger and provides plenty of visual interest.

either on a concrete base for vehicular weights or a more pliable road base mixture for your average daily human traffic. The only other questions you need to concern yourself with are the number of grout lines you want and which direction the pattern should run across the space.

TURF is a traditional favourite but it needs a steady supply of water, regular fertilizing and pesticide to keep it looking good all year round. I tell my clients, if you have kids then it's probably worth it, but otherwise I would always prefer to see a space filled with a rich spread of plant life interrupted by paths and niches,

platforms and decks. It's simple really: you're creating a garden because there's something about nature that you like, but a lawn all but defeats that purpose by flattening the original landscape and covering it over.

STONE comes in a multitude of fantastic textural finishes such as honed (an unpolished matt surface with a sheen), bush-hammered (an even surface studded with pocks for grip and texture) and split-face (a roughly chipped, highly uneven surface). Then there are all the wonderful reconstructed stone like terrazzo where crushed aggregates are bonded together in concrete and polished back to give a great retro look.

ECO TIP

Pebbles have become hugely popular in the garden, but to be honest, I question where some of them come from. I was a big fan until I started doing research on where they originate and was horrified to discover that many tons are lifted off beaches and pulled out of riverbeds in countries where water is in short supply. You see, pebbles are one of nature's filtering systems, and if they are removed from an already struggling waterway, the liquid that remains quickly becomes rank and contaminated. So if you're covering a large area, please think about using them conservatively by mixing them in with other surface materials (like recycled concrete, for example) and avoiding the piled-up look. Lately, I've started encouraging people to use crushed stone rather than pebbles. Quartz, granite, sandstone or recycled crushed concrete are just some of the great-looking alternatives available.

CREAMY CLAY TILES look fantastic against pale greys and delicate blues – colours that remind us of a crystal ocean and pristine sandy beach (left). EXTERIOR TIMBER FLOORS (centre) weather and age with the changing seasons, and can provide a strong visual link between indoors and out. PONTOONS SLOW DOWN the viewer, encouraging us to take a bit more time observing the surroundings. This gently undulating pontoon pathway (right) picks its way through a carpet of groundcovers, spot-planted shrubs and sunken sleepers.

THE OWNERS OF this comfortable Federation
home wanted to get rid of the struggling lawn
which took up most of their outdoor area, so the
small paved section of split-face sandstone which
had aged to a lovely soft grey was extended to
become the dominant ground surface. As you can
see on the following pages, when the sandstone is
new it's a much paler beige, but with time and
weather it will end up blending with the old
section. Garden beds were built up in keeping with
the existing green-scape which has a distinct
tropical flavour. The result is a leafy array of lush
shade- and moisture-loving species.

Cool and elegant, stone brings an aura of luxury and opulence to any room, but you need to carefully pick the areas where you use it. Honed stone is dangerous as a pool surround because of its slippery finish, and a delicate glass dropped on stone will shatter into a million tiny shards that could haunt your entertainment area for months. Food and drink on an unsealed surface can lead to stains, with red wine a major culprit. A careless splash of shiraz will leave an everlasting pink reminder.

CONCRETE is a versatile, inexpensive contemporary surface, and when finished in the right way it can look very impressive. There are lots of ways you can alter the texture and it takes colour brilliantly, but make sure the pigment or oxide is mixed directly into the concrete rather than painted on top as surface paint wears quickly,

especially in busy areas. One of my favourite finishes is exposed aggregate, where the concrete is sprayed with a high-pressure hose before it has fully cured, washing away the top layer and exposing the flecks of stone or aggregate in the mix.

CERAMIC tiles can be a stunning focal point, but I usually use them in covered spaces because once water gets onto a tile you're skating on ice. The same goes for glass and resin. Generally installed in sheets or tile form, they are an expensive option so better to use them as a highlight material (especially in conjunction with light and water) rather than the main event.

WOOD is one of the most neutral, controllable materials you can get your hands on. Cool in summer and warm in winter, it's deliciously tactile and is one of the only surfaces you can picture yourself lying on

LAWN

AGAPANTHUS UNIT PAVING COLOUR BLUESTONE

STONE EDGE

25-30MM BLACK POLISHED PEBBLE

CANNA LILLIES

TIMBER PONTOON DECKS

A SERIES OF differently shaped overlapping decks descend through this outdoor room, with the timbers laid in various directions to guide the eye towards special points of interest in the garden.

wearing a pair of swimmers without a towel in between. There are thousands of neglected timber decks out there giving wood a bad name, but minimal maintenance is all it requires to serve you well for many years. It's a myth that wood doesn't cope well in the elements – trees come from outside, after all. Once the timber is cut it continues to breathe, expanding and contracting with the seasons, so you simply allow for that by nurturing it like any other living organism. Think of it as just another growing element to the garden that requires feeding and maintenance, and like a well-kept plant, it will pay you back many times with its soft healthy glow, silky smoothness underfoot, and strength and durability.

Treated pine is a plantation timber that responds beautifully to stains and oiling. (A quick tip is to buy boiled oil which is

free of the organisms that cause mould and mildew patches.) There are different ratings of treatment to be aware of before you buy: H5 means it can be immersed in fresh water, H4 means it can be sunk in ground. All treated timbers are vermin-proof and will resist mould and rot. Remember that once you cut it, you must re-treat the exposed portion with a preserva-tive like copper napthinate, because even the smallest untreated area opens the way for potentially damaging organisms to spoil the whole piece.

And finally, when decking planks are assembled, ensure they have at least 3mm gap between them. A timber deck will buckle, warp or split only when the boards are banked up too tightly against each other, much like a wisdom tooth grows through the gum and forces the other teeth forward.

favourite growing floors

Well, I've told you already how I feel about lawn, but there are some fantastic low-maintenance groundcovers that really shine in small spaces or as complementary borders for bricks and pavers.

Ajuga reptans 'Atropurpurea' (Bugle Weed) has a dark, lush, burgundy foliage.

Pratia pedunculata (Matted Pratia) is flat and fine-leafed with tiny white or blue flowers.

Ophiopogon japonicus (Mondo Grass) forms soft, spiky dark-green clumps.

Heterocentron elegans (Spanish Shawl) has a vivid pink flower and fine green leaves making it an attractive two-toned cover.

Sagina subulata (Pearlwort) is spongy and robust with a fine-leafed surface.

Dichondra repens (Kidney Weed) forms a clover-like carpet.

Soleirolia soleirolii (Baby's Tears) is delicate and mossy and grows well in shade.

Grevillea 'Poorinda Royal Mantle' (Royal Mantle Grevillea) is a thick, rambling groundcover which is great for stabilising banks.

Hardenbergia violacea (False Sarsparilla) has a long dark-green leaf and a delicate purple flower.

Viola hederacea (Native Violet) is soft and clover-like with tiny purple and white blooms.

LEFT TO RIGHT: Dianella *sp.*, Carpobrotus edulis, Loropetalum *'Burgundy'*, Ajuga reptans.

THERE'S A SUPERB *atmosphere of cosiness and*
wellbeing in this courtyard, and the floor surfaces
have a lot to do with the success of the overall
effect. Slabs of sandstone cut into random
geometric shapes are laid in simple, ornamental
form, bringing a light, reflective quality to the
shady space. Smooth decking breaks the sandstone
into mini arenas, banding the garden beds and
echoing the solid bench seat which faces a small
fountain trickling from the hollowed centre
of a block of lava stone. With sturdy rendered
brick walls, there's a pervading sense of privacy and
security so the owners can relax completely and
enjoy the full benefits of their outdoor room.

THE LARGE-FORMAT *floor slabs resonate with the chunky blocks of this low retaining wall. The key here is the strip of timber that divides vertical and horizontal sandstone, emphasising the marriage of identical materials but very different textures.*

SLEEK AND SMOOTH *to the touch, this stretch of timber platform (below left) glows warmly under low-voltage lighting. A variety of timber widths introduce a subtle decorative element, proving once again that with a little imagination there is tremendous visual potential in a simple wooden surface. Well-concealed lighting illuminates the pond (below right), a radiant miniature stage draped in a forest of gilded leaves and stems.*

THIS VIEW ENCOMPASSES *much of what I love about the outdoor room. With the doors folded back, inside and out dissolve into a single, wholly livable space. Carpet becomes wood becomes sandstone becomes plant. The plain timber desk and chair match the timber bench, and puddles of directional light bathe the chosen points of interest, uniting all facets of the interior and exterior. Note the storage space that complements rather than intrudes. The lofty timber cupboard pictured behind the glass door holds all the bulky garden equipment and conceals the obligatory water meter.*

FLOORS
inspiration

CHAPTER THREE THE FURNISHINGS
HOLD THE BODY, PLEASE THE EYE

This is where creativity really kicks in. With all the structural elements in place, the next step is to introduce the magnets that will entice a body to sit or recline or dine, the containers that will present swatches of living colour and texture, and all the extras that will make the outdoor room as comfortable and convenient as the rooms inside.

For many, presentation is the main focus. As a visual person I can thoroughly relate to this, but I would never sacrifice functionality for aesthetics, especially when it comes to a much-used living area. The trick, as always, is to find the right balance, and I have a simple theory with which I've had overwhelming success: the more you can design in situ that's permanent (like built-in benches), the better the space will look all year round. It's just like having a permanently made-up bed. Alternatively, design your commodities and

equipment so they can be easily folded up or tucked away. More and more of my clients are asking for tables that can be swung up and stored flush with the wall, freeing up valuable space. And custom-made furnishing always looks that little bit more attractive because it's unique to the location.

There's a lot to be said for gardens that only require minimal maintenance, and for people with busy lives it may be a necessity, but I think owners who eliminate the need for any upkeep whatsoever are missing out. Even the simplest task is a creative act: from tending a small tub of flowers to oiling a wooden deckchair. When you actively care for your garden it becomes more valuable and you don't take it for granted. Even the smallest chore means you've invested in the space – it's become part of your life – so I love to see owners interacting with their garden.

PLACING PEOPLE

Positioning the various pieces in your outdoor room is as straightforward as furnishing your loungeroom. Identify the main feature (water, accent plants or sculpture draws the eye just like a television), and arrange your seats and lounges at the best vantage points. Then make your adjustments according to where the sun falls throughout the day, perhaps rigging up a bamboo blind to shield a swing chair from afternoon glare or shifting the breakfast table so it's bathed in morning light. Similarly, don't put the main point of congregation in an exposed area: nothing is worse than being blown about or being cooked in the midday sun while you're trying to eat a meal or read the paper.

Take note of the outlook from each position and ensure that no-one winds up staring at a blank wall. And instead of forcing everyone in the dining area to sit at the table all the time, try to arrange it so that one end snuggles up against some informal bench seating so people can move there for more intimate conversation before and after eating. Even better, corner niches are a great chat zone, and you should fully exploit all the corners or right angles in your seating formation so that people can interact face-to-face.

I make no apology for being a rabid promoter of bench seating – it is without doubt a signature part of my outdoor rooms. A free-standing armchair eats up lots of precious space, whereas benches are part of the perimeter itself. Benches are the best way to keep the space looking clean and uncluttered. They are sleek and immovable so you can maintain your original style forever which is a great way of policing the design integrity and ensuring that it remains true.

ALTHOUGH THIS BENCH is lowered by what looks to be a negligible amount, it's a significant level change that entices the viewer to sit or recline. Hinged at one end, it tilts into an adjustable backrest which can be softened with cushions and bollards stored within the bench void. Yuccas (Yucca elephantipes) *are uplit to make the most of their starburst foliage, and the spot-planted Baby's Tears* (Soleirolia soleirolii) *will quickly spread and join up to form a mossy groundcover.*

BENCH SEATING

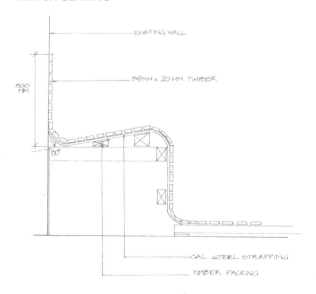

AT NIGHT YOU can really see how levels play a major part in every aspect of this outdoor room. The effect is intimate yet spacious, and the furnishings are discreet and versatile.

THE DELICIOUS MAGNOLIA (left) and frangipani flowers (right) smell almost good enough to eat. I love their creamy petals, and the rosy spectrum of colour within the frangipani reminds me of a tropical sunset.

A bench is far nicer to look at than a retaining wall, and it introduces a new level that softens the hard vertical angle of the sheer face. Best of all it's a great magnet, a place of rest that gives people a reason to go out there and appreciate what the room and garden beyond have to offer.

Lumbar support is a bit of a preoccupation of mine, not only because I'm concerned about back health, but also to encourage people to feel they can sprawl out. In custom-made benches I'll insert a small timber support-dome in the slats about 220mm up from the base of the bench. Cushions are optional but can bring a lovely tactile element. Their colours also help theme the room, and a vividly exotic Thai fabric or striking tribal print might become the decisive unifying element. Marine canvas is one of the hardiest fabrics, but you

can experiment by waterproofing other fabrics. Log cushions are a good alternative where a bench design doesn't include built-in lumbar support.

Though it will cost more to build, hinging your benches so that the tops flip up revealing voids for useful storage is a brilliant way to maintain the original look of the space. And you can tuck cushions out of sight whenever they're not in use, ensuring the cushion fabric will have a longer life.

If you don't want to go all the way and use built-in benches, think about the width of the capping on your retaining walls. Design them no lower than 420mm or higher than 550mm and between 450mm and 600mm wide and you have a handy surface for seating, display and numerous other purposes.

SUNKEN SEATING

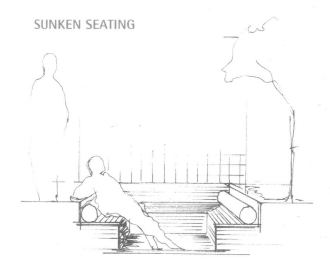

STRONG, CLEAN LINES, *simple planting and a sense of space and elongation was the brief for this narrow courtyard. To divert attention from the overlooking apartments, a water feature extends along the boundary. The liquid trickles from emitters at the top and slides across slender resin shelves which look particularly attractive lit up at night, taking on a faintly luminous quality.*

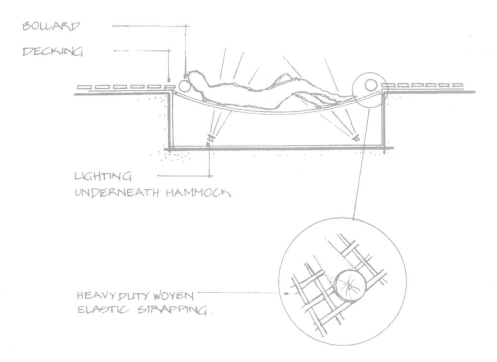

BOLLARD

DECKING

LIGHTING
UNDERNEATH HAMMOCK

HEAVY DUTY WOVEN
ELASTIC STRAPPING.

It's not hard to spot that I love the look of metal and wood together. Man-made alongside organic is far and away my favourite combination of materials. Timber and metal are contemporary and classic all at once and when brought together the resulting piece doesn't need dressing up so it retains an air of wholeness and simplicity. They are so very different, that a marvellous balance occurs so I feature them a lot in my custom-made furniture.

Metals that are ideal for outside include marine-grade aluminium (cast or extruded), and the top-notch finish of stainless steel. Avoid mild steel unless you are deliberately after an ageing or rusted look. It should be powder-coated or galvanised and you must cap the bottom of the object because whatever it sits on (pavers, stone, etc.) will rub back the surface so the steel will eventually corrode and bleed rusty streaks.

I tend to use timbers like tallow-wood, ironbark, teak, cedar, turpentine, kwila and treated pine, but take note that they must all be looked after to some extent. Shellacs, sealers and estapols give strong protection but they lock in the moisture so the wood may eventually crack or chip and you'll have to sand it back and start all over again. I prefer to feed the wood with an oil like tongue oil or teak oil (a pre-boiled product without impurities) which is thin enough to penetrate the grains and nourish the wood while still letting it breathe.

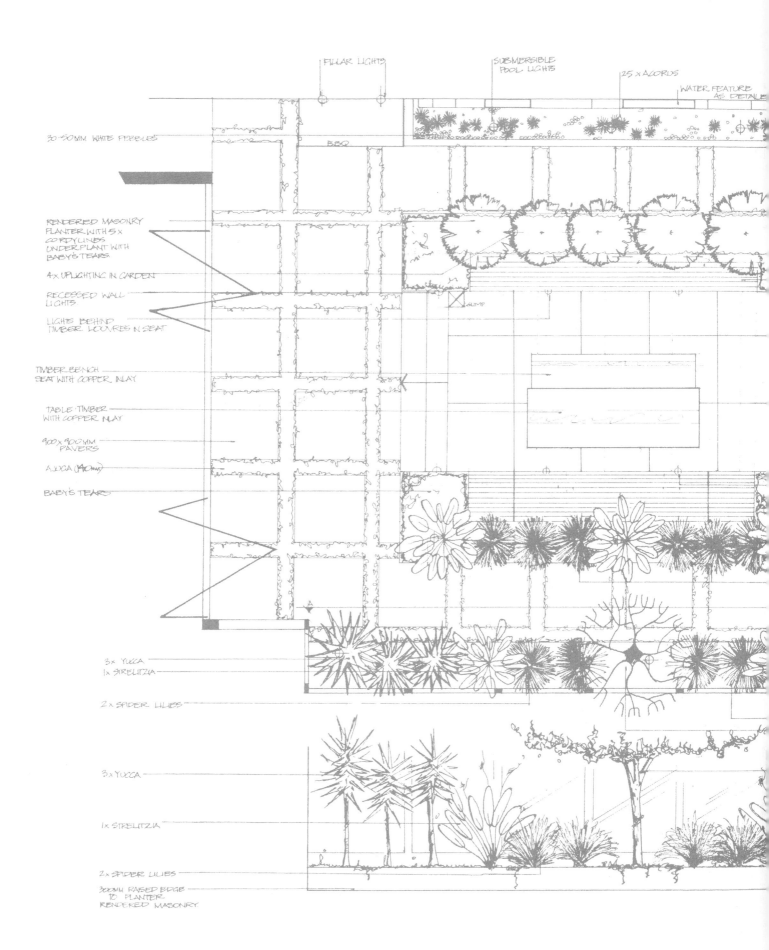

PILLAR LIGHTS

SUBMERSIBLE POOL LIGHTS

25 x ACORUS

WATER FEATURE AS DETAILS

30-50MM WHITE PEBBLES

BBQ

RENDERED MASONRY PLANTER WITH 5 x CORDYLINES UNDERPLANT WITH BABY'S TEARS

4 x UPLIGHTING IN GARDEN

RECESSED WALL LIGHTS.

LIGHTS BEHIND TIMBER LOUVRES IN SEAT

SUMP

TIMBER BENCH SEAT WITH COPPER INLAY

TABLE TIMBER WITH COPPER INLAY

900 x 900MM PAVERS

AJUGA (40MM)

BABY'S TEARS

3 x YUCCA
1 x STRELITZIA

2 x SPIDER LILIES

3 x YUCCA

1 x STRELITZIA

2 x SPIDER LILIES

300MM RAISED EDGE TO PLANTER RENDERED MASONRY

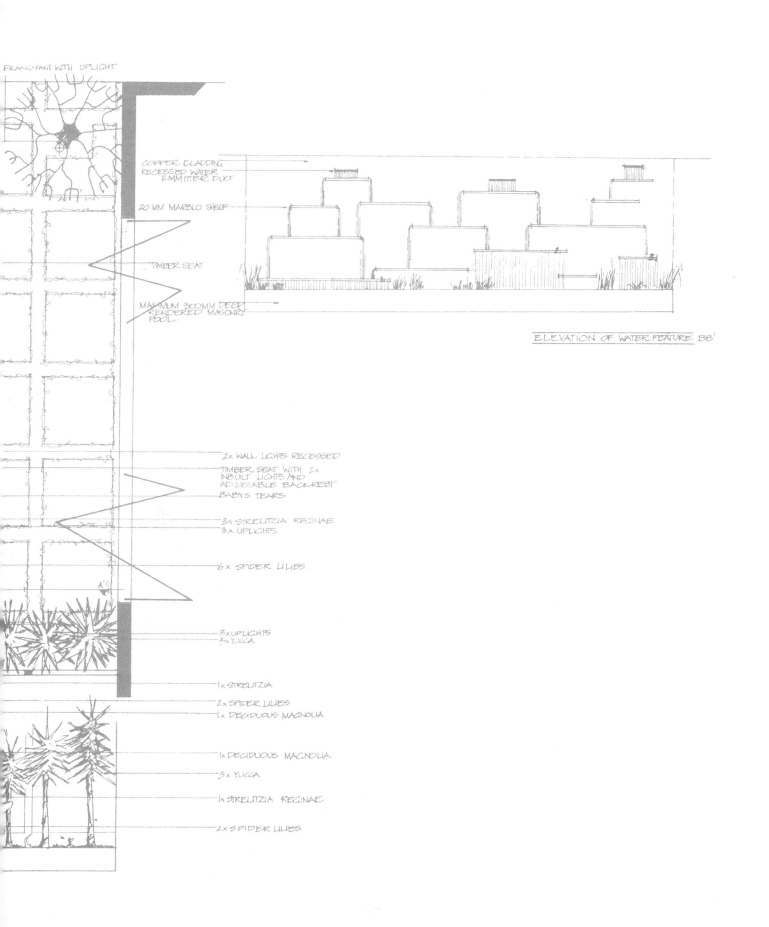

FRANGIPANI WITH UPLIGHT

COPPER CLADDING
RECESSED WATER
EMMITTER DUCT

20 MM MARBLO SHELF

TIMBER SEAT

MAXIMUM 300MM DEEP
RENDERED MASONRY
POOL

ELEVATION OF WATER FEATURE BB'

2x WALL LIGHTS RECESSED
TIMBER SEAT WITH 2x
INBUILT LIGHTS AND
ADJUSTABLE BACKREST
BABY'S TEARS

3x STRELITZIA REGINAE
3x UPLIGHTS.

6x SPIDER LILIES

3x UPLIGHTS
3x YUCCA

1x STRELITZIA

2x SPIDER LILIES

1x DECIDUOUS MAGNOLIA

1x DECIDUOUS MAGNOLIA

3x YUCCA

1x STRELITZIA REGINAE

2x SPIDER LILIES

THIS BRIGHT, AIRY balcony needed lots of greenery to interrupt the stark white lines of the base structure. An elevated spa takes full advantage of the tranquil outlook of treetops and sky, while bathers are protected from the wind with a clear glass barrier. To permit all-important drainage, the whole area has a slight incline, so the portable bench seats and tables have been custom-built with adjustable feet to compensate for the slope. Cushions on the planter bench-seat can be removed to make way for a food preparation and serving space when catering for large numbers. The balcony is furnished with elegant stainless steel and timber custom-made furniture (below left), and to complement them, custom-made triangular wall-pots (below right) with ascending containers that hold a cascading display of hardy annuals and succulents.

A MODERN INTERPRETATION *of a traditional*
Japanese water spout (right). Although usually
made of bamboo, this one is stainless-steel. The
steady flow pours from a bluestone catchment to
the glass pond beneath brimming with plants and a
family of fish. Against the bold, clean lines of a
timber fence on the other side of the balcony,
clumps of ox-eye daisy, flax and Echeveria *are a*
striking contrast in rambling free-form (below).

LATTICE TRELLIS

4 x OSTEOSPERMUM 'WHIRLIGIG'

2 x PETREA VOLUBILIS

H x CLIVE

7 x ACME

SPA

A ▲

A1 ▲

DECKING

DOOR TO UNDER DECKING

STEPS

STEP LITES ½ WAY UP RISER

LIGHT

GATE

LIGHT

SEAT (1500MM)

5 x ACMENA SMITHII VAR. MINOR

1 x AGAVE ATTENUATA

10 x OSTEOSPERMUM 'WHIRLIGIG'

1 x ANIGOZANTHOS

1 x AGAVE ATTENUATA

SEATS (1500MM) (SEE DETAIL)

1 x ANIGOZANTHOS

1 x AGAVE ATTENUATA

WATER FEATURE (SEE DETAIL)

BBQ (TO BE DETAILED)

LIGHT (")

BENCH TABLE (")

SEAT (1900MM)

5 x ACMENA SMITHII VAR. MINOR

1 x AGAVE ATTENUATA

2 x OSTEOSPERMUM 'WHIRLIGIG'

1 x YUCCA IN POT (POT BY CLIENT)

OVERHEAD STRUCTURE (EXISTING)
SHADE TIMBERS NOT SHOWN (SEE SPECS)

EZYDECK (AT CLIENTS' OPTION)

STRIP DRAIN

STEP LITES - INSTALL ½ WAY UP WALL

LIGHT

LIGHT

1 x YUCCA IN POT (POT BY CLIENT)

SEAT (1900MM)

6 x ACMENA SMITHII VAR. MINOR

1 x AGAVE ATTENUATA

2 x OSTEOSPERMUM 'WHIRLIGIG'

SEAT DETAIL
Scale 1:10

SATIN PERSPEX PANELS
- FIXED AT ALTERNATING
LOCATIONS ON THE 5 SEPERATE
BENCHES - SEE A - E

STAINLESS STEEL BOX SECTION

19 x 35mm KARRI TIMBERS

10 ~ 35

50

200

50

150

A

B

D

E

50   50

485

566 TYP

150

1900
(OR 1500 AS INDICATED ON PLAN
WHERE DISTANCE BETWEEN LEGS TO BE 433MM)

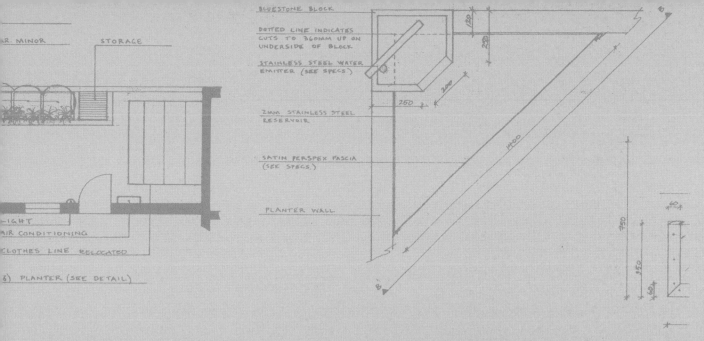

BLUESTONE BLOCK

DOTTED LINE INDICATES
CUTS TO 360MM UP ON
UNDERSIDE OF BLOCK

STAINLESS STEEL WATER
EMITTER (SEE SPECS)

2MM STAINLESS STEEL
RESERVOIR

SATIN PERSPEX FASCIA
(SEE SPECS.)

PLANTER WALL

AR. MINOR

STORAGE

-IGHT

AIR CONDITIONING

CLOTHES LINE RELOCATED

6) PLANTER (SEE DETAIL)

250

1.2 × 2.4.
9 1800
12 1800
12 2400.

ON/ELEVATION AA

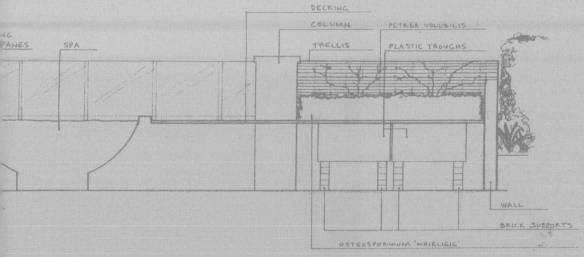

DECKING

COLUMN   PETREA VOLUBILIS

TRELLIS   PLASTIC TROUGHS

NG
PANES

SPA

WALL

BRICK SUPPORTS

OSTEOSPERMUM 'WHIRLIGIG'

BROMELIAD PLANTER
Scale 1:10

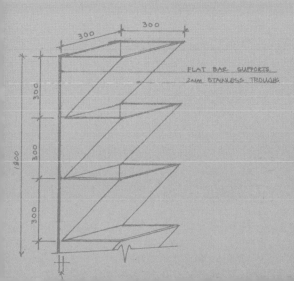

300   300

300

300

300

1800

300

FLAT BAR SUPPORTS
2MM STAINLESS TROUGHS

PLANT SCHEDULE

BOTANICAL NAME	COMMON NAME	SIZE	QTY.
Acmena smithii var. minor	Lilly Pilly	25L	23
Agave attenuata	Agave	45L	5
Anigozanthos 'Bush Dawn'	Kangaroo Paw	8IN	2
Osteospermum 'Whirligig'	Whirligig Ox-Eye Daisy	6IN	18
Clivea miniata	Clivea	8IN	14
Petrea volubilis	Purple Wreath	8IN	2
Guzmania (cv with burgundy in leaves)	Bromeliad	8IN	6
Yucca elephantipes	Yucca	45L	2

CONTAINMENT

Customised planters are great for filling small or awkward spaces or simply because you want something totally original. I have commissioned fabricators to build planters out of stainless steel, copper, marine-grade aluminium, zinc, plastic and resin, but there are impressive new products appearing on the market every day. Recently I was blown away by some fantastic angular zinc pots from Paris and a couple of thick white plastic urns from Italy that made a stunning focal point in an ultra-hip inner-city courtyard.

If your choice is a permeable substance like reconstituted sandstone, terracotta, concrete, stone or brickwork, be aware that they are porous and will heat up and suck all the moisture and nutrients from the soil – in effect, competing with the plant. This can be overcome by having the surface glazed, so it is less porous and no longer leaches the soil.

When you purchase from the manufacturer, check there are drainage holes in the base – you'd be amazed how many of them neglect this. Make sure the container is large enough for the amount of soil needed to sustain the plant, and if the plant has a large canopy, the pot should be heavily anchored by the weight of the earth or the wind will tip it over.

Design with shapes when you're choosing your foliage: tall and elongated, squat and robust, spiky, feathery, fleshy – think about its

ECO TIP

Any receptacle – and I do mean any – can be adapted into a planter. Become a scavenger like me and you'll look at back sheds, council dumps and hard rubbish days with entirely new eyes. Recycling materials is not only positive from an environmental point of view, but you may also unearth a unique work of 'found art' which infuses tremendous character and personality into your outdoor room. Old metal rubbish bins, tyre parts and discarded wine barrels are just some of the so-called waste materials that have been reclaimed and restored to become quirky, clever and inspiring conversation pieces.

impact on the overall effect. A shrub or small tree that needs a lot of water and fertilizer will struggle in a pot, so go for hardy varieties like flaxes, *Lomandra longifolia*, arum lilies, *Dietes*, yuccas, dracaenas, cacti and succulents, and any of the palms. Also think about which part of the plant is the most attractive: do you want the foliage to be eye height or would you prefer to look down on a canopy of leaves? This will be determined by the size of the container so make sure the pot fits the plant.

PLANTS WITH STRONG shapes work well in containers. Succulents are often a great choice, particularly these spiky agaves. Aloes (centre) or Kalanchoe (right), while Canna 'Tropicana', with its more traditional leaf shape and burnished copper hue, makes an arresting contrast plant.

CONTAINERS
inspiration

Please don't expect the same soil to feed a plant forever. When re-potting, you need to carefully pull the plant out, gently loosen up the root ball, add fresh potting mix and settle it again. Potting mixes have a world of nutritious additives these days: water-saving crystals, slow-release fertilizer, wetting agents, drainage aids and trace elements. The health of your pot plant depends almost entirely on what goes into this mix so don't skimp by settling for the cheaper brands.

It's always a good idea to twist pots around every two to three weeks so sun reaches all parts of the plant and you maintain a healthy, even growth. And the pot should be elevated at least 20mm off the ground so it can drain freely and be easily hosed under. You can use anything you like for this but a couple of pebbles or small stones make sturdy little pedestals and they don't cost a cent.

BITS AND PIECES

Colour and ornamentation are as important for the outside as for the inside, and here's a good way to start thinking about the choices you'll make. Walk through the house observing your fabrics, pictures, the shapes of chairs and vases, jewellery and light fittings. Most of these things can be interpreted in some way for an outdoor setting and adapted to endure the elements. Style-wise, this makes the passage from inside to out a far more seamless transition and promotes a feeling of harmony and completion.

The market for outdoor furniture and equipment is booming. Every luxury, it seems, is catered for, from state-of-the-art sound systems to projection gear for home cinema. I'm all for bringing technology outside but take care not to go overboard: an excess of noisy diversions like television, video and computer games can destroy the unique ambiance of an outdoor space. Focus instead on integrating those little indulgences that lend themselves to a natural environment, like a hammock to rock away a lazy afternoon or a handsome stone chess set for marathon family tournaments.

A SIMPLE, SOLID wooden bench performs well in a busy garden (left). WITH AN EVER-INCREASING array of new furniture styles and materials on the market, the traditional timber bench seat (centre left) remains a fine choice for positions such as this one submerged in a verdant bank of Teucrium. BUILT-IN FURNITURE CAN give you flexibility: rope handles are the only things that give away the large and very useful storage space within this bench (centre right). AN INTENSE SPLASH of colour (right) demands attention and soft, bulky padding invites comfort and repose.

WORKING WITH RATHER *than against this rolling landscape, a pontoon trail of 'mini-platforms' rises up with the land to serve as lookout points, then drops down with the fall of the land providing stepping-stones to cross a small stream. Moving back towards the house, the path steps up to a retaining wall and resolves itself in a daybed that can be cushioned for a snooze in the sun or just perched upon for a contemplative breather (below left). Because there was a lot going on at ground level, it was important to provide a vertical contrast to balance things up. Large upright ornamental timbers were placed at random intervals (below right) and suddenly the garden took on a whole new, almost monumental dimension.*

TIMBER AND STONE are a pleasant tactile contrast and offer visual diversity as the eye picks its way along the track. Edging this property is a belt of dense bushland so the pontoon trail eventually peters off into the landscape beyond like stepping-stones into the wilderness.

inspiration
FURNISHINGS

for art's sake

Art is such a personal thing, but whatever your taste, I can't emphasise enough how pivotal an art piece can be in placing your individual stamp on an outdoor room. It enhances your feeling of pride and ownership and brings character and personality to the space. You might choose a dry sculpture or a custom-built water feature, you could construct an arrangement of timber on the wall, a mosaic design on the floor or paint a mural on the fence – the possibilities are endless.

If you're having trouble settling on a medium, I would suggest that stone sculpture works stunningly just about everywhere. Classic and timeless, this ancient material radiates a solid immortality that gives the garden a sense of longevity and eternal character. I have long been awed by the monolithic stone circles like Stonehenge and Avebury that dot the English countryside. They are inspiring on a purely aesthetic level but are deeply spiritual, too. Scottish artist Andy Goldsworthy is someone whose work I admire enormously. He is celebrated for imposing startling contemporary designs on a wide range of organic materials and erecting them in vast natural landscapes. This is the essence of what I strive to do in my work every day.

The best advice I can give you is to follow your gut instinct. I can't lead you in any one direction because I truly believe that art should be a reflection of yourself, but perhaps this will help: my most adored personal piece of art is my Yogi. A simple wooden sculpture of a man crouched into a ball, he comes with me every time I move house and is one of the few possessions that I'll never part with. He always looks so peaceful, so well rounded, so symmetrical and yet so solid … to me he symbolises what I struggle to be every day as a person.

I hope you find your own Yogi.

'AS LONG AS YOU CHOOSE WISELY,
A TREE CAN BE THE BEST SCULPTURE YOU EVER
INVEST IN ... AN EVER–CHANGING ART PIECE
WITH ITS OWN SCULPTURAL AGENDA.'

CHAPTER FOUR THE
KITCHEN
FEEDING AND FEASTING

Laughter, conversation, sharing, nurturing: these are all things I associate with cooking and eating outdoors. Food is a huge social magnet. Families and friends congregate around the table in anticipation of being fed, building relationships and celebrating the joys of togetherness – and it all seems that little bit more special when experienced in a natural environment.

Isn't it funny how food seems to taste better outside? I like to think it's a primal memory buried deep in our psyches that dates back to a time when our ancient ancestors cooked and ate around an open fire. Whatever the reason, people of all cultures continue to be drawn to the flames and I get a buzz every time I see a

tiny inner-city balcony almost completely taken up by the prized barbecue. Such dedication!

Let's not forget that it's great for male bonding: once blokes step out the door and grab the tongs it's suddenly okay to cook. But these days the outdoor kitchen is not just about the ubiquitous barbie. More and more of my clients are asking for the same amenities outside as they have in their indoor kitchens and I'm more than happy to oblige. Being outside separates you somehow from normality, giving you a kind of holiday from the everyday. What luxury to be fully set up when you're cooking outdoors. I promote whenever I can the novelty of having everything at your fingertips.

THE GREAT AUSSIE OBSESSION

So many choices in outdoor cooking facilities are available now, there really is no excuse for an ugly piece of equipment which looks awkward and out of place. If you customise your barbecue and work to blend it in with the theme, it becomes part of the garden and not just an afterthought, so respect it as you would a key piece of furniture. I'll generally select the model in close consultation with the client and purchase it without a stand. Then together we take the time to choose appropriate cladding and cover it in a way that echoes the style of the whole room. Apart from aesthetics, customising your barbecue also saves space, allowing for benches on either side and cupboard space beneath.

A few dos and don'ts about positioning: never seat diners so close that they might be spattered by fat or have smoke billowing in their faces. Keep it as far away from windows as possible and ensure that the hotplates are well lit for night-time cook-outs. At the same time don't place the culinary action away from the sitting area. It's important for the chef to participate and, let's face it, food preparation is a wonderful conversational tool. A big part of the pleasure of the outdoor cooking and eating experience is to make sure everyone's involved, either helping set up the meal or mucking in with the cleanup.

Try to place your cooker beneath a wall that will act as a barrier in case things go wrong gas-wise, and if your gas bottles are exposed at all, make sure doors are locked when children are around. (Rule number one: gas and kids don't mix!) And while you're at it, check that sharp utensils and any breakables are under lock and key, just as they would be in the inside kitchen.

A DINING TABLE emerges smoothly from the timber deck and then vanishes into a single plane, freeing up precious space. Designed by Patio team-member David Vago, this small courtyard off an inner-city terrace is full of great solutions to the outdoor dining dilemma. Once the table is raised into place, the surrounding deck is transformed to become in situ bench seating with rattan cushions trimmed in Chinese silk. A shallow rill of water embraces a portion of the dining area and, softly illuminated with spills of light, it becomes a velvety liquid carpet when night falls.

AH – THE BARBECUE *in action! This unit was
purchased without a stand and installed with brick
and timber surrounds, blending seamlessly with the
overall theme. High barriers on two sides act as
safety walls, and plenty of bench space puts
condiments and implements within easy reach.
Best of all is the proximity of chef to diners, which
allows the free flow of conversation and ensures
the tantalising aroma of food being prepared whets
everyone's appetite.*

Stainless steel and sealed granite are a popular choice for benchtops because they require minimal grout and their non-porous properties guarantee that foodstuffs won't stain them. When not in use, these surfaces can double as stands for small pieces of sculpture or other ornamentation. Splashbacks to the rear of the cooking plate are a must as well as being a fine opportunity for accent colour. Fix a shelf along the splashback and you have condiments and utensils within easy reach while you prepare the meal. Utilities like sinks and fridges are easy enough to install and, as for outdoor cookware, the sky's the limit. Basically, if your crockery and implements can withstand the punishment dished out in an average kitchen, then they can withstand whatever the outdoor elements throw at them, too.

WHERE THE HEARTH IS

It's a great feeling being outside in the wind and weather on a chilly afternoon but you're snuggled up and warm as toast. Outdoor heaters seem to be everywhere these days, particularly in those parts of the country with a cooler climate. For smaller spaces like courtyards and balconies, wall-mounted heaters are safe and very effective. Then there are the hooded umbrella-style heaters which have really taken off in the last few years because they are safe, self-sufficient with their own gas bottles, and easy to move around. You'll see them outside cafes and restaurants in the winter months, bringing in the business and lots of cosy customers. It's just another part of controlling your environment out there by customising it to suit yourself. The more comfortable you make your outdoor room for every circumstance, the more you're going to use it.

GATHER ROUND

Most outdoor rooms and courtyards are geometrical by nature so I prefer the table to be geometric, too. For this reason, you'll see the majority of the tables in my garden designs are rectangular, allowing for the greatest diversity in seating arrangement. Benches are another story altogether and you can really go to town experimenting with voluptuous curves, but tables need to fit into L-shaped seating designs so that you can cater for large numbers if need be.

NEUTRAL-COLOURED WALLS *are a calm background for randomly criss-crossed stands of Black Bamboo with its unmistakable clumps of massed foliage and smatterings of fragile leaves.*

In the interests of comfort, benches should be 450mm to 600mm wide and 420mm to 550mm high. When you place the table, there needs to be no more than 150mm between the edge of the table and the edge of the bench. Any further away and diners have to lean in too far to reach their plates; any closer and it starts to get a bit tight squeezing in and out, which is especially problematic for the less mobile among us.

AN EDIBLE GARDEN

There are few things more satisfying than being able to reach out and pluck your own ingredients straight from the soil. Growing food and flavourings is easy and you don't need much room: even the smallest flat can have a mini herb garden. Start with a humble window box on a sunny sill, fill it with chives, basil, coriander, dill and parsley, feed it regularly and change the soil every six months or so, and you're in business.

For larger spreads it's all about location. The bed or planter needs to be in the right spot – out of the wind but with plenty of sun – and it should be raised to a good height so you don't have to bend down far to tend to it. A smorgasbord of vegetables planted in clever formation will produce a brilliant ornamental mass that easily rivals any flower display.

As attractive and welcoming as wood burners can be, sadly they are no good for the planet because wood smoke is high on the list of greenhouse emissions. They're not so good for the human respiratory system either, because the high particle emission is known to trigger asthma attacks. Your best bet is to go for gas heaters and take comfort in the fact they are a clean and cost-effective burn.

I love clusters of curly endive, cherry tomatoes, chillies (especially the Thai varieties) and basil all crowded together in a glorious edible mess. Clumps of herbs make neat, frilly borders and spread rapidly into fragrant groundcovers. Garden beds framed by rosemary hedges look fantastic, with the added bonus that when you brush the leaves as you pass, a marvellously fresh and subtle scent is released.

If you're thinking about including edibles in your plant landscape, there are some definite stand-outs that look as good as they taste. Pineapples are an arresting accent plant with their striking architectural form, while passionfruits are brilliant for climbing and screening (*Passiflora edulis* will fruit more if you train it to climb laterally). Cumquats bring forth gleaming little orange orbs and hold their shape well, especially when they're hedged or topiaried. You can't go wrong with the tangy scent of lemons and oranges and the dwarf varieties grow exceptionally well in pots. Apples have a delicate blossom and lustrous crop and pears with their distinctive shapely fruit prosper in cooler climates. Strawberries are a sweet and abundant groundcover, and pumpkins and zucchinis thrive in hot spaces. I've always had a soft spot for edible flowers, too. My mum sprinkles bright splashes of marigold in her legendary salads, and my grandma in Sri Lanka used to slip nasturtium leaves in my sandwiches for a little extra spice.

SKETCHES ARE GREAT for identifying whether different shapes will work in the space. Here we see how kidney-shaped (above), oval (top right) and linear furnishings play a dominant role in each of these outdoor rooms.

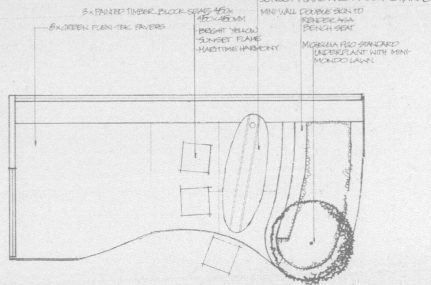

SURFBOARD SWINGING TABLE· MARINE PLY 1700×600 MM
SUNSET FLAME AND MARITIME HARMONY

3 × PAINTED TIMBER· BLOCK SEATS 450×
450×450MM

MINI-WALL DOUBLE SKIN TO
RENDER AS A
BENCH SEAT

8× GREEN FLEXI-TEK PAVERS

-BRIGHT YELLOW
-SUNSET FLAME
-MARITIME HARMONY

MICHELLIA FIGO STANDARD
UNDERPLANT WITH MINI-
MONDO LAWN

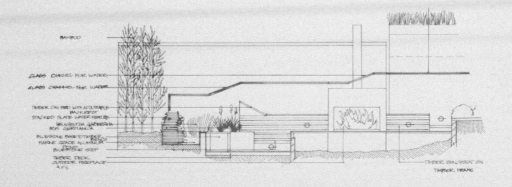

BAMBOO

GLASS CHANNEL FOR WATER
GLASS CHANNEL FOR WATER

TIMBER DAY BED WITH ADJUSTABLE
BACKREST
STACKED SLATE WATER FEATURE
WITH BUDDHA GARDENIA
IRIS GERMANICA
BLUESTONE BASE/TIMBER
MARINE GRADE ALUMINIUM
GRASS
BLUESTONE STEP
TIMBER DECK
OUTDOOR FIREPLACE
AFS

TIMBER BENCH SEAT ON
TIMBER FRAME

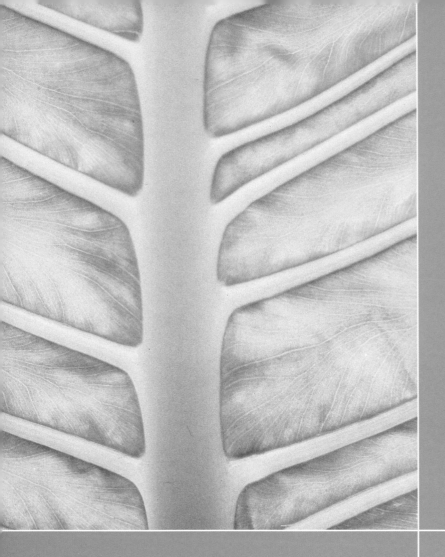

COLOUR
inspiration

into bloom

You might not think it, but I absolutely adore flowers. The trouble is, most of the challenges in my work involve large-scale architectural constructions and the smaller decorative touches come long after I have left the scene. Given the space, the sun and the time, I will jump at the chance to get stuck into the floral side of things. In the past I've had the privilege of designing landscapes for several country gardens and I love the freedom of playing with different forms of foliage and thoroughly satisfying my green thumb.

In the outdoor room, a shapely pot or urn looks wonderful filled with masses of dazzling colour. Anything with strappy, upright foliage is good: November lilies and day lilies make an arresting statement, as does *Strelitzia reginae* (Bird of Paradise) whose structure makes it one of the best accent plants for a courtyard space. Don't forget bulbs and the joy they bring, particularly to children. Vivid clumps of daffodils and clouds of perfumed jonquils are a glorious annual event and the exquisite cups of tulip flowers are the embodiment of spring.

GREVILLIA SERICEA *(top left)*, Banksia spinulosa *(rop right)*, Strelitzia reginae *var.* juncea *(above)*, Aechmea fasciata *(facing page)*.

CHAPTER FIVE THE
BATHROOM
ULTIMATE CLEAN

Do you remember the first time you went skinny-dipping? For me the occasion was at an isolated billabong in north-western Australia when I was nine years old. There was nobody else around apart from me and some mates so we dared each other to lose the swimmers and all jumped in together. At first I felt incredibly exposed, but then I started to relax and gradually became suffused with a strange kind of energy. There's something amazing about moving through water with nothing but the sky to cover you, feeling very much a part of the natural world.

Of course, there aren't too many opportunities in the city to take an outdoor dip au naturel. I associate that kind of experience with holidays – an empty beach, private spa or secluded waterhole. How

fantastic to be able to recreate that sensation in your own home: soaking in a hot tub on a cool evening, surrounded by lush plants and a velvety sky above, staring at the moon … makes you smile just thinking about it!

Then there's the experience of bathing with a friend or four. In my mind, eating together is a lot like bathing together. Just as food is a reason to congregate and build relationships, so is water a relaxing place to gather and talk and share. In ancient Rome, the public baths were important social centres where business was conducted, friendships made, and news and gossip exchanged. In this country of water-lovers, I think it's a great shame that a culture of communal bathing never took off, but an outdoor bathroom must surely be the next best thing.

rain room

'I'll never ever forget my first trip to Bali when I signed up for a massage in a 'rain room'. For close to an hour my body was gently pummelled until I tingled all over, then the masseur stepped out and activated a system of sprinklers criss-crossing the ceiling.

The room began to rain!

The delight of that afternoon has stayed with me and made me determined to find ways of reproducing a similar kind of experience for my clients whenever budget allows.'

SHOWER POWER

Time and again I've installed an outdoor shower and the client will say to me months later that they use it far more often than their indoor facilities. So look out – you might get addicted!

The beauty of it is that you don't need a lot of space. As long as your walls are high enough, the only other basic requirements are a shower rose and adequate drainage that empties into the stormwater system. If you prefer to feel more enclosed, there's everything from folding glass shutters to a mass of upright screening plants to hinder prying eyes. Much depends on the prevailing theme but I would try to use, as always, a natural material which is more tactile and welcoming against bare skin.

The floor for the shower area must be able to withstand blasts of water and prolonged periods of dampness. A series of treated timber dowel batons fixed in a row gives adequate grip and feels good under wet feet. Pavers should have a matt finish and be slip-resistant. A slab of porous stone is fine, as long as it is in a position where it can dry in the sun. If polished or honed stone is the main floor surface in your outdoor room, the shower area must be completely surrounded and separated from the rest so that water isn't walked across the floor or doesn't accidentally drain into the living area and make it a slippery hazard zone.

As for the green screen, any water-loving plants – such as papyrus – will thrive in the moist atmosphere.

BUBBLE-TUBS AND MINI OCEANS

Once upon a time spas were a true luxury item, found only in the homes of the very rich and the very decadent. Now anyone can install their own kit spa: the plumbing is included so the cladding and surrounds are all you have to worry about. Decking is my preferred surface because it's non-slip and maintains an even temperature as well as being soft on the feet and beautiful to lie on with bare skin.

If you are fortunate enough to have a view from your outdoor room, position the tub or spa so that whoever is using it can take full advantage of the natural vista. By the same token, if there is no outlook to exploit, then create one – a special feature for the eye to rest upon while the body enjoys a long, bubbly soak.

Swimming pools are the supreme example of bringing your holiday back home, symbolically recreating the seaside in a domestic domain. Like all other elements of the outdoor room, a pool can be dressed up to become the main focus for indulgent activities. Recently I saw a pool that typified how a simple addition to the pool area can make it look extravagant and luxurious. Deliberately sunk beside a well-established avocado tree, the deck was built around the foliage so you could just reach up and pick the fruit from its lush, laden branches. Talk about indulgent!

When I design pools, I always aim to include enticements for people to linger once they've had their swim. The wet edge is an innovation I've begun to use, where a shallow indent runs along the entire length of one side. A sheet of water gently sluices over the lip, cooling sunbathers with a sensual trickle so they feel they are still immersed in the main body of water.

THE PILLAR WATER feature consists of random-split slabs of grey slate. Water emerges from a slit near the top of the pillar and slides silently down the pearly grey surface to replenish the channel beneath. The narrow rill that embraces this tile expanse instantly cools the space and provides a flicker of constant movement. Light timber pontoons lie across the rill, allowing access to the bench seats either side of the pillar where the sitter might choose to dangle hot feet in the delicious cool. A fine finishing touch is the glass mosaic edge of muted blue-grey tiles.

THIS LARGE COURTYARD *is constantly in use so it's important for the owners to be able to clear the decks for the next activity. The barbecue (left) is mobile so can be stored in the corner, and there is an icebox beneath the tiled benches. Other benches conceal the entire water-filter system. It's a canine paradise – and pretty good for the human occupants, too! With a couple of energetic water-loving pets like Stoli and Tiger, the owners were delighted with this shallow dog-safe mini-pool running along the boundary-line (below).*

*HIGH TIMBER WALLS snuggle up to a bank
of dense foliage with enough privacy for an
unscreened shower which is used far more
frequently than the home-owners expected. And
who can blame them? The wooden deck feels great
underfoot (with spaces between the slats for good
drainage), there's lots of lush greenery to enjoy, and
the timber screen provides sufficient privacy while
still revealing a pleasing view of the garden beyond.*

Any pool will dominate a backyard, so great care should be taken with its visual presentation, no matter what size. Turquoise is inevitably associated with tropical locations so it's a great colour for pool interiors, but I've seen black, slate and even red pool interiors that look magnificent in gardens with a strong contemporary flavour. Just remember that the darker the pool colour is, the smaller it will look, and in those cases where there is a lot of high shadowy foliage around it, the inky depths can look positively forbidding.

There's no avoiding the ugly accompaniment of plastic coils and boxes of filter gear, but I've come to see that disguising the pool cleaning system is an opportunity to introduce interesting new structures into the outdoor room. Think of the pump housing as a striking level change: a ready-made stand for pots brimming with lush plant life, its sides perhaps festooned with creepers.

The texture of the finish will often be a big factor in determining the amount of maintenance you'll need to keep your pool sparkling clean. Pebblecrete finishes look natural and feel pleasant underfoot but debris can settle and stubbornly cling to them. Smoother surfaces like epoxy paints on rendered concrete are low maintenance because they don't attract grime and are easy to vacuum. As a bonus, concrete can be dressed up with a continuous panel of mosaic tile on the skim-line which, when colour-matched, ties in with the general theme of the outdoor room.

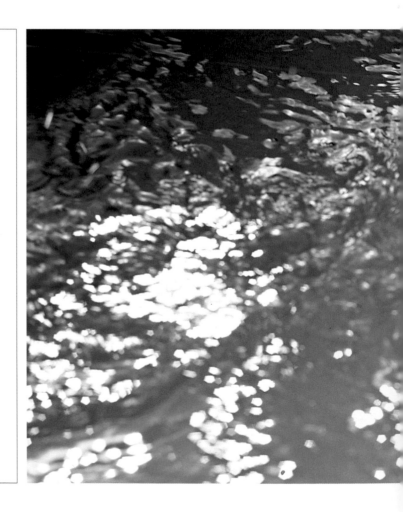

A DENSE STAND of bamboo makes a great screen to protect your privacy in an outdoor bathroom. Here you can see that with stripy bamboo (centre) the beauty is in the detail. There's no doubt about it: when it comes to patterns, nature wins hands down every time. Another beautiful – and rare – bamboo is Giant Timber Bamboo (Dendrocalamopsis oldhamii, overleaf). And when it comes to sun protection, nature also provides. This giant elephant's ear (Alocasia macrorrhiza, right) is an attractive and effective sunshade.

'HALF THE PLEASURE
OF THE OUTDOOR ROOM IS
NURTURING WHAT'S IN IT.'

a fantasy...

One day the outdoor room will be a standard
part of every Australian home, just like the
kitchen or living room is now. I can almost
picture the real estate advertisements in the
Saturday papers:

*'Solid brick family home comprising three spacious bedrooms, family
room, formal dining, bathroom, kitchen and meals area, laundry, fully
functioning outdoor room and landscaped garden plus OSP ...'*

*'Two-bedroom apartment, spacious lnge and dining with north-facing
balcony room and fountain, eat-in kitchen, sep laundry, central htg
and LUG ...'*

*'Beautifully located 2BR Victorian conceals 3 bright liv/din spaces
including outdoor room with kitchenette and tub ...'*

A CONTEMPORARY VERSION *of the backyard tub. Black-stained timber, offset with polished pebbles, leads up to the bath, where the bather can lie back and study cloud formations for hours on end (or at least until the water goes cold). A mulberry-coloured curved wall takes care of nosy passers-by, with a tall screen of copper strips and bamboo poles painted a luscious tomato-red to provide visual relief against its solid expanse. In the foreground are mounds of glossy* Hebe, *while the lawn section (below) descends in curved terraces, held in place by copper strips that echo the dominating screen at the rear.*

Clients often come to me with an existing pool that they want to look new again. Merely surrounding the area with a new surface (like timber decking) and extending a length of coping down into the water will transform it completely.

And finally, whether you are renovating or building anew, make sure the surfaces surrounding the pool echo the surfaces in the outdoor room. Too many materials create visual boxes, so keep it simple and the pool will not look separated from the rest of the garden.

The old claw-footed tub doesn't require any kind of barrier but spas and pools that are permanently filled with water must be fenced off by law. Check with your local council for the specifics, but generally fences must have self-closing doors with locks or latches that are too high for children to reach and need to be at least a metre away from all other climbable constructions and boundaries. Any lateral slats or bars within the fence structure are illegal.

Fence costs vary, with the frameless glass barrier hovering at the top of the range and the standard powder-coated aluminium bars one of the more popular cheap options. Both fulfil the safety obligations and both look good in the right situation.

To avoid the feeling that you are 'caged' by the fence, dot plants around the perimeter. Any Australian species that survive the so-called front line salt tolerant areas (ie coastal) are better for around pools, including *Scaevola* and *Westringia*.

SETTING THE SCENE

Now for the finishing touches. There are so many simple, cheap and effective ways to promote an atmosphere of pleasure and repose around water. Candles need no justification: they are a compulsory addition to any meditative or romantic situation and you can never have too many. The delicate scent of incense or oil burners, the golden flicker of an ornate lantern, the melodic tinkle of wind chimes all foster a restful ambiance. For a truly indulgent bathing experience, sprinkle aromatic flower petals on the surface (try rose petals, geranium petals or my all-time favourite, frangipani).

inspiration
BATHROOM

WATER IS AN all-pervading presence in this beautiful harbourside home, and what better way to introduce the theme than this dramatic entranceway with its lush stand of Strelitzia nicolai on one side and a glassy lap pool on the other. A quick after-swim rinse in the poolside shower, and bathers are ready to move on to the spa bath out the back with a spectacular uninterrupted view down to the sea.

WATER FEATURE
IT'S ELEMENTARY

If you want to create a garden that is truly whole, you must include as many natural elements as possible. Again, this is an idea that stems from the Japanese tradition of a garden as a miniature landscape, and you'd have to agree no landscape is complete without an ocean, a river or a glittering ribbon of water running through. This is just one of the reasons why I believe it's so important to have some kind of liquid source in your outdoor space.

When people ask me why I am so passionate about water, I just say, 'Me and twenty million others!' Australians are predominantly coastal dwellers. Whether we live in sight of the ocean or not, we are inevitably drawn to the water.

It's just our way. We choose to have our holidays there, our weekends, we go there to escape, to unwind, to regroup. Is it any wonder then that more and more of us seek to bring some kind of symbolic reminder of this experience into our personal living spaces?

I always encourage my clients to include water (most don't need much convincing), and it invariably ends up being the prime sensual focus, stimulating sight, sound, touch, smell and even taste (if you want to go that far). Cool, clear moving liquid refreshes the soul, it's a superb tool for relaxation and is perfectly in keeping with my philosophy on what the outdoor room should provide.

THE JOURNEY

Building a water feature is a science and it can be a major structural operation so the decision to include one needs to come early in the piece. First you must establish if there's an appropriate place for it. Will it be seen to its maximum advantage? Do you want a single jet or a system of meandering waterways to trail around the space like a unifying thread? Will it be incorporated into levels or run beside pathways? Is there a vantage point that allows it to be seen from inside as well?

Don't be discouraged if your outdoor room seems too small – there's always a place for water. You can run a skin of water down an existing wall, hover an elegant tap over an ornamental basin or install a system of rills around the perimeter. Be aware of the noise factor in a smaller space: loud splashing in close proximity can be very irritating, so avoid long falls of water and keep the pressure down low. On the other hand, the gurgle of running water can be a blessed antidote to the intrusive hum of background urban noise.

Keeping children's safety in mind, I'll usually build the reservoir, cistern or balance tank well out of reach of curious little ones. In the case of exposed water like open streams or cascades, the run will only be 50mm to 60mm deep, so kids can interact without being in any danger.

THERE'S A DISTINCTIVE contemporary flavour in this terrace house, and the aim was to take the feeling outside to the tiny courtyard which opens directly onto the main living room. A feature wall of stucco plasterwork (overleaf) was painted Porter's 'Library Red' to contrast with the white smooth render. Five stainless-steel disc-shaped emitters spurt even jets into the stainless-steel rill, a movement echoed by sprays of Xanthorrhoea *(Grass Tree, right). Pots of* Crassula *and* Kalanchoe *(left) echo the disc shapes with their plump round leaves.*

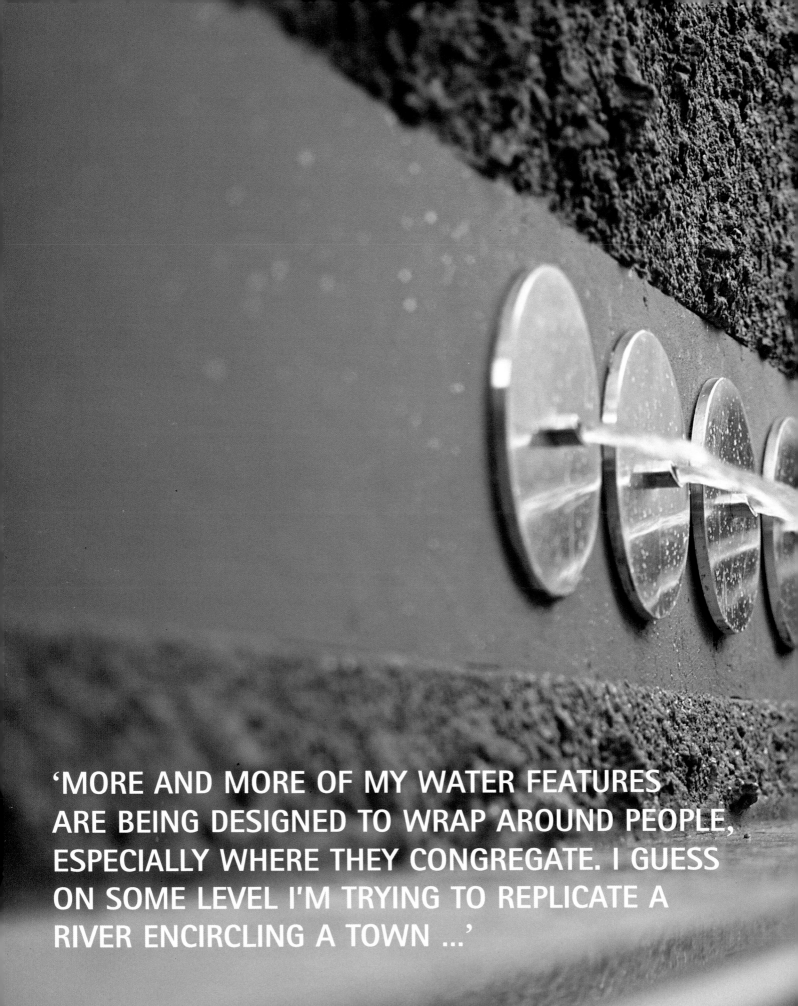

'MORE AND MORE OF MY WATER FEATURES
ARE BEING DESIGNED TO WRAP AROUND PEOPLE,
ESPECIALLY WHERE THEY CONGREGATE. I GUESS
ON SOME LEVEL I'M TRYING TO REPLICATE A
RIVER ENCIRCLING A TOWN ...'

There are some hard and fast rules that apply to all spaces. Water needs sun shining on it for at least part of the day or mosquitoes may converge and breed. It also needs to be protected from drafts and breezes, as wind promotes rapid evaporation and your water levels will soon deplete. The colour of your catchment pond or vessel deserves some careful consideration. A bright, light shade is fine for shallow runs but a more substantial catchment looks great in a darker shade. Not only does it increase the illusion of depth, it also acts as a mirror, reflecting the plant life around it and the sky overhead and it conceals unsightly debris, mould and tannin stains from falling leaves. Finally, keep as much of the mechanics concealed as possible so the eye is drawn to the actual fall of the water and not the place where it ends up. In simple terms, allow the viewer to focus on the journey more than the destination: it's the movement of the water that is exciting.

AQUA INTERRUPTUS

On its own, water seems passive to the naked eye. It only comes alive when it interacts with something, becoming dynamic as it responds to what's around it. I will rarely run water over a surface without some kind of interruption and this is where the interest comes in. The challenge is to ensure that the water doesn't kick off the obstruction and spray outwards; it needs to calmly leave and return to the main surface with smooth ripples, not moisture-guzzling splashes.

Because I design so many water features, I'm always searching for new waterproof materials to work with and new ways to make them interact. Glass, stainless steel, brass, stone, perspex and resin are materials I frequently turn to, and I'm endlessly fascinated by what water does to metals like copper, forcing it to adapt and to age naturally by oxidisation.

IMPORTED FROM TURKEY, this graceful marble basin feature with its elaborate filigree tap is an exotic addition to a shady rustic garden. The visual clincher here is the clever use of colour which sets the contemplative mood. Dark green foliage from next door peeps over the wall to find complementary hues in the deep purple taro plant or Elephant's Ear (Colocasia esculenta 'Black Magic') nestled in the basin. Uniting the palette is the rendered wall painted a soothing slate blue and deliberately distressed so the base material shows through with varying texture and patches of salt damp. The effect is one of timeworn charm, classic design and a hint of faraway places.

THE BRIEF FOR *this major project in the entranceway of an interior design centre was for a natural, free-flowing, safe and unobtrusive installation in breezy neutral tones. Limestone and glass are the base materials: a combination which to my mind works in faultless harmony with the reflective qualities of water, especially when lit up at night.*

SLABS OF BROKEN *limestone sandwiched between broad planes of glass make up the vertical component of the feature. Water rises in a slender channel carved through the centre of each stone 'mountain', seeps down its waved edges and across the rippled stone terraces at the base before finally disappearing in the narrow crack, where it is recycled and begins its journey once more. The whole structure is slightly elevated so people · can sit on the rim and dip their fingers in. Children love this 'big pond' and it's perfectly safe for them to interact. I'm a firm believer that you can find inspiration absolutely everywhere. The carved stone mounds in this feature (detail overleaf) came directly from memories of playing with an ant farm when I was a kid. In my travels, I've been lucky enough to see the real thing: dramatic ant-hills towering like metre-high monoliths in the Australian desert. I'm reminded of their haunting beauty and the hive of industriousness within whenever I look at this.*

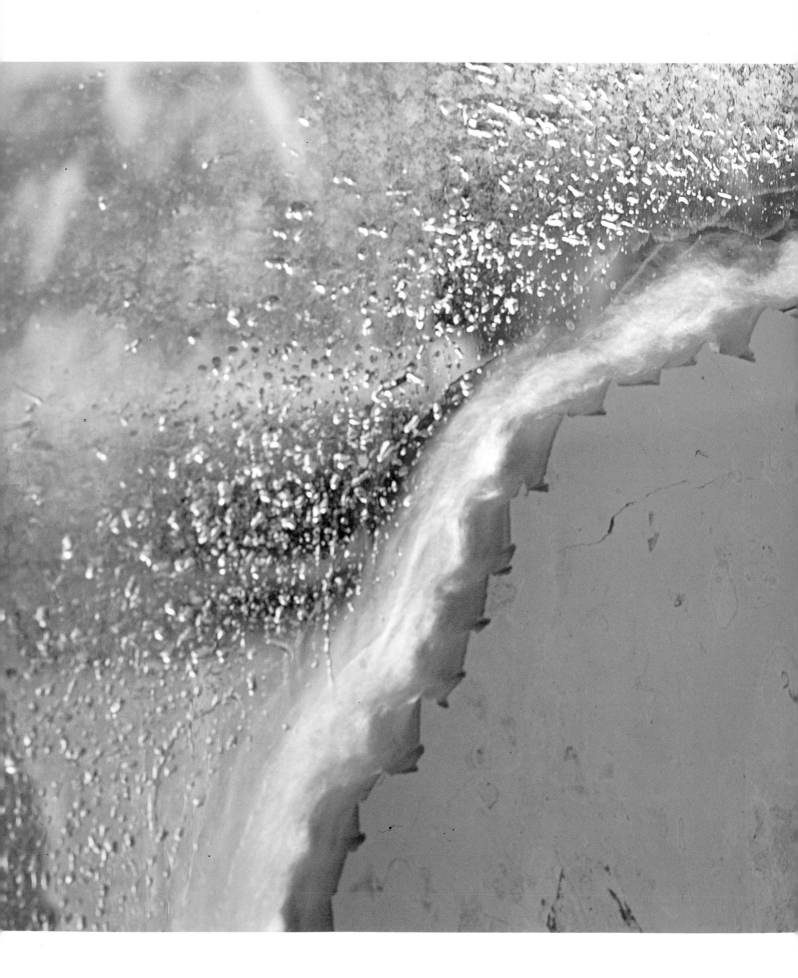

I've seen wonderfully intricate water constructions made with branches of driftwood, pieces of pottery and crazy twists of scrap metal, as well as catchments from every conceivable waterproof vessel under the sun. So whatever you do, keep an open mind and be prepared to give anything a go.

DO THE RIGHT THING

In these days of shortages and restrictions, water is very much at the forefront of environmental concerns. Every feature will lose a small amount of moisture, but in most cases the water is fully recycled, and water features don't consume water and nutrients as a large plant taking up that same space would. A still body of water has calming, reflective properties but generally it's desirable to have a degree of turbulence so the liquid constantly oxygenates, making it fresh and clean. Keep in mind the fact that the slower it moves the less evaporation will occur, and a free-falling cascade will often splash or be carried by the wind, losing precious moisture.

GREEN WATER WORLD

I don't think I've ever met a water plant I didn't like. I guess that's why the features that appeal to me most are the ones that use fresh water, replicating wetlands or marshes on a much smaller scale. I like the idea of introducing a body of water where a frog or a fish or a bird can interact – particularly in the middle of a city where a natural oasis is a rare sight.

Water evaporation is costly and wasteful, so be diligent in checking that the reservoir is absolutely leak-proof and that *all* the water ends up in the reservoir or pond at journey's end. Free-falling water evaporates quickly, so let the water slip over an interim surface rather than having it fall directly from source to destination.

A JAPANESE WATER spout – in stainless-steel rather than bamboo – spills water into a glass pond (left). AS NATURAL AS can be, a single plume bubbles in a shallow bowl carved into a block of sandstone encircled by nodding leaves (centre). WATER SPRAYS FROM between overlapping sheets of cor-ten (right).

These days I'm doing a lot of multi-tiered waterfalls with short drops from level to level. Each catchment is filled with its own miniature eco-system made up of a variety of bog plants like Sedge (*Carex*) and Rush (*Juncus*), bulrush, *Isolepis nodosa* and *Helmholtzia glaberrima* (Stream Lily). They naturally help filter the water, they look great, and some species even discourage mosquitoes.

Other plants that thrive in a watery environment are arum lilies, Louisiana Iris, *Nymphaea*, *Acorus gramineus* and, of course, the ever-versatile papyrus. But I must admit to a huge bias towards the stunning lotus. Every incarnation of this plant looks sensational, from the seed pods to the unopened buds to the bird-like flowers. In fact, I love them so much that the logo for my design business is based on a stylised lotus shape.

A final tip: water plants are generally quite hardy but they will struggle if the water is polluted or if they have been planted too deeply. When too much of the foliage is underwater, the plant is prevented from photosynthesising and it will eventually die.

MAINTAIN THE SPARKLE

Happily, water features are very easy to maintain once they've been installed correctly. Here are some useful trouble-shooting tips.

An OVERFLOW PIPE about 30mm in diameter should be installed in every pond about 20mm above the water surface to prevent overflow and flooding.

AUTOMATIC FLOAT-VALVES are nifty little gadgets available from irrigation suppliers that help keep the water at an even level.

AN AUTHENTIC MOROCCAN design hand-carved in sandstone, this unusual wall-fountain emanates character and charm. A healthy Ficus pumila (creeping fig) paints the wall behind a deep emerald hue to blend with what is already a very green space. The pond below is edged with bagged brickwork and softened by a cluster of arum lilies. Opening directly onto this view is the master bedroom, so the owners are greeted every new day by this blissful sight.

DISCOURAGE MOSQUITOES by ensuring there is some sort of movement in the water and that sun shines directly on it for part of the day. You can also add salt or chlorine to the mix, and plants like *Helmholtzia glaberrima* are excellent insect turn-offs, too.

TANNIN from fallen leaves will cause discolouration, so avoid planting trees and shrubs close to the basin or pond.

BIO-FILTER is an innovative new cleaning system which provides a home for good bacteria to work on breaking down the toxins that build up in the water.

RULES AND REGULATIONS vary with different councils around Australia, but generally, a body of water should be no deeper than 300mm or else it must be surrounded by a pool fence.

FOR PLANTING IN and around water features, or even in damp areas, choose plants that enjoy a moist environment, like this giant elephant's ear (Alocasia macrorrhiza, left). Bromeliads (centre and right) thrive in a moist, humid atmosphere, but need good drainage for their roots.

ALONG ONE SIDE of this inner-city terrace, a small, dank, cupboard-like void was transformed into a water-room with a distinctly modern edge to match the stylish interior of the home. Walls were clad in stone, and long vertical glass louvres were fixed at carefully spaced intervals. Discreet emitters dispense a steady stream down the glass panes into a shallow pool below, which is filled with black pebbles that conceal the unsightly pump and pipes.

teamwork

Everyone has the capability to create an exceptional outdoor room. And like any creative enterprise, it's always good to get other people involved once your plans start to take shape. I can't count the number of times I've walked into a garden and immediately picked out things that lend themselves to a theme only to have the owner admit that it had never occurred to them. The simple truth is you can't help but take your own place for granted, especially if you've lived there for a while.

Without my colleagues at Patio, my design concepts would remain just that. They are the ones who spur me on, support my ideas and help provide the technical expertise to make my designs a reality. I'd be lost without these guys – they've been an indispensable touchstone throughout my creative journey.

So don't be afraid to bounce ideas off someone else, whether it be a professional designer or a trusted friend. Remember there really is nothing like a fresh eye: it's easy, it's clever, and it helps you take full advantage of what's right in front of you.

inspiration
WATER FEATURES

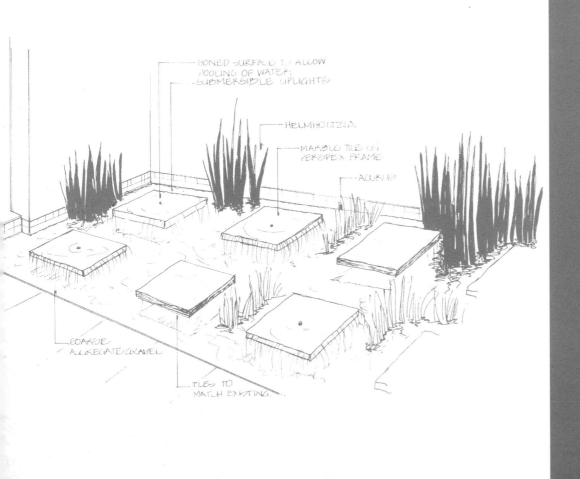

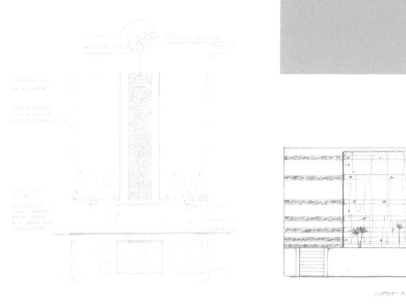

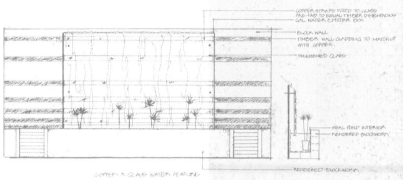

COPPER & GLASS WATER FEATURE

ORN/POT (BY CLIENT)

SUPPORT - SIZE DEPENDS
ON POT.
CONCRETE PAD & STRIP
FOOTING
150mm GRAVEL

POND WALL 500mm ↑

ADJACENT GARDEN

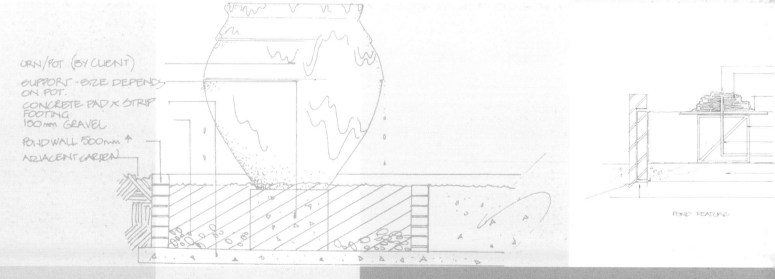

POND FEATURE

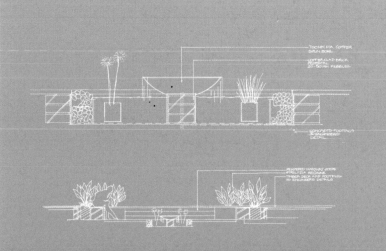

CHAPTER SEVEN LET THERE BE
LIGHT

Well it just goes to show, you can take the boy out of Vegas, but you can't take Vegas out of the boy! For nearly a decade I was based in that glittering city in the heart of the Nevada desert, famous for its frantic nightlife and gargantuan electricity bills. There's no better place to learn about stage illumination, and I spent a lot of my time designing complex lighting rigs for theatre and cabaret shows that went on to tour the world. After Vegas, designing light for gardens feels like child's play. The principles are exactly the same: I'm still lighting a subject, still concealing the light source and still controlling the size of the beam, it's just the 'stage' is a lot smaller and the 'stars' don't do much dancing!

Where budget allows, the lighting design is one of the more enjoyable aspects of my work.

It's also something I feel very strongly about. Without lighting, you're denying yourself the pleasure of your outdoor room at night and, for people with busy working lives, this is often their only opportunity to take advantage of the space during the week. One of the things I find myself saying to clients time and again is, you've paid for your domain, so why not ensure you can use it every hour of the day and night?

There's a magical quality to a well-lit garden. Light instantly transforms the space, highlighting features that are barely noticeable during the daylight hours and transforming the atmosphere with the flick of a switch, from soft and intimate to vivid and theatrical. This is a wonderful opportunity to let your imagination run wild.

GETTING TECHNICAL

Don't baulk at the prospect of playing with lighting because it looks too technical. Believe me, the rudiments are easy to grasp and it can end up being one of the most fun, creative and satisfying aspects of planning and building your outdoor room. Here are some basic starting points for you to think about:

PLACEMENT My golden rule here is that the source should always be discreet. Don't get me wrong, there are some great-looking fittings around, but be careful they don't end up dominating – the focus should be on the garden and not the lighting fixture. Probably the most common lighting mistakes people make are to do with placing the light itself. For example, an up-light might be positioned too close to the subject, lighting only a small portion of it. And front-lighting the subject tends to wash out all of the subtle detail. If you light the same piece from the side, above or below, it suddenly comes to life and develops an interesting third dimension.

DIRECTION To maximise the architectural potential of a subject, think beyond the standard in-front lighting. Consider a side-casting light, drawing attention to a particular section of a wall or a hedge. This can look amazingly effective, throwing up wonderful shadowy shapes. Pillar lights that shoot a striking vertical beam are an excellent choice for an entrance or a wall, but be sure to place the light source at eye level, otherwise it will be uncomfortably dazzling for the observer.

BY DAY A MEDITATION pavilion partially screened by decorative awnings and engulfed in masses of varied foliage. At night, softly coloured lights create a scene of romance and mystery.

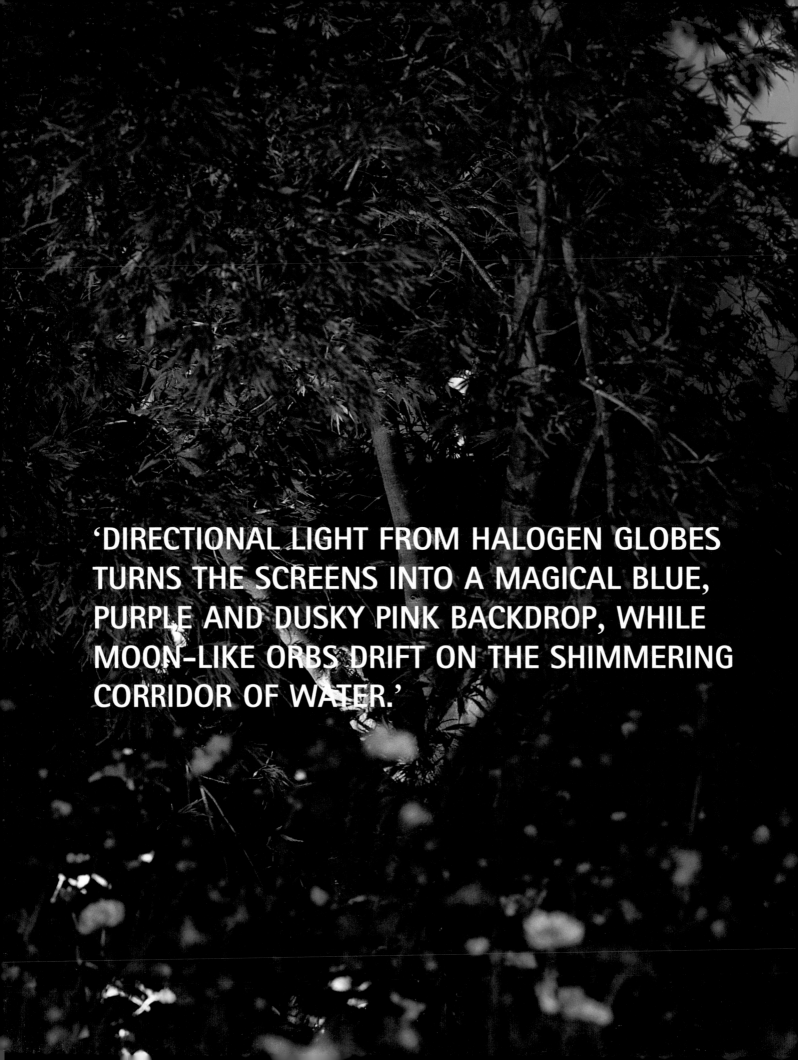

'DIRECTIONAL LIGHT FROM HALOGEN GLOBES TURNS THE SCREENS INTO A MAGICAL BLUE, PURPLE AND DUSKY PINK BACKDROP, WHILE MOON-LIKE ORBS DRIFT ON THE SHIMMERING CORRIDOR OF WATER.'

INTENSITY This is all about the strength of the lights. You need to ensure the beam will travel far enough to light the subject in its entirety. In simple terms, we're talking wattage, so this factor will come into play when you're choosing your globes.

FOCUS I'm a big fan of low-voltage lighting because the globes come with a projecting angle of anywhere between 13 degrees (a directional pin-spot for small subject) and 65 degrees (to flood a hedge or tree). This gives you the opportunity to pour the focus on a particular object to the exclusion of all else. Great for the star features.

COLOUR Have you ever wondered why 24-hour convenience stores are awash with the bright white light of fluorescent bars? This is a deliberate ploy to deter 'undesirables' because stark illumination is not welcoming (some would say it's downright hostile). And how about the lights in dressing rooms? We've all experienced the harsh and unflattering effects of a white wash when we're trying

clothes on, whereas softer, warmer hues are far more forgiving and attractive. Well, the same principle goes for lighting your garden. This is why I tend to go for halogen globes or fibre-optic tubes which work well not just because of their low intensity and soft glow but also for the wonderful variety of shades they offer. If you decide to go for colour, the choice can be extremely important. Consider the mood you want to create and always remember that subtlety is the key. Too much variety can wind up looking tacky unless you are making a bold, contemporary statement and even then you have to be very sure of what you're doing. I've always favoured blue for its mysterious, underwater feel and warm, buttery yellows seem to go well anywhere. As a rule of thumb, try to choose colours that already occur naturally in your garden and complement these existing tones rather than using colours that contrast and undermine them. My best advice is to go for one, or maybe two basic tints, and follow a unifying theme throughout the space.

WHEN DARKNESS FALLS this rooftop really comes into its own, offering a great venue for parties. Light from the inside, enhanced by the reflection of a treacly timber floor, spills through cantilevered glass doors and louvre blinds. Rows of downlights take care of the immediate deck area, and directional spots shooting across tubs of wildly sprouting grasses set the mood for those wishing to have a quiet chat away from the centre of action. A borrowed lighting landscape is provided by city buildings twinkling merrily against the night sky several kilometres away.

THE LARGE-FORMAT *timber platforms on this rooftop are sunk in a bed of washed pebbles that were created by tumbling rocks rather than mining river beds. Each pontoon is a different size to break up the rigid formal lines of the ground plane. Slatted timber screens inhibit strong gusts of wind while still revealing the city views in the distance. Baby Sun Rose* (Aptenia cordifolia) *tumbles from a row of window boxes (left).*

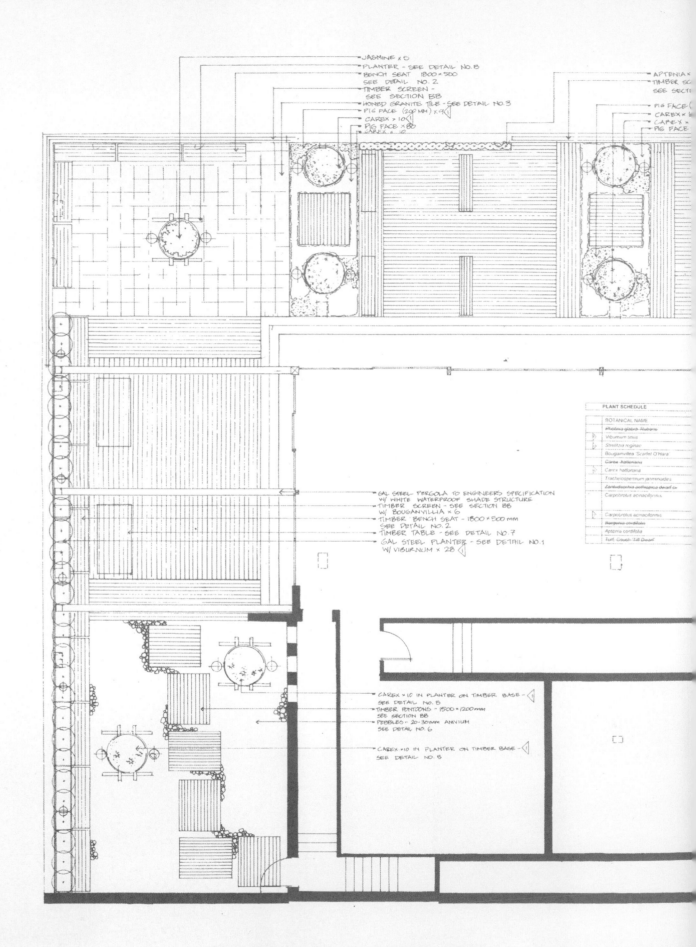

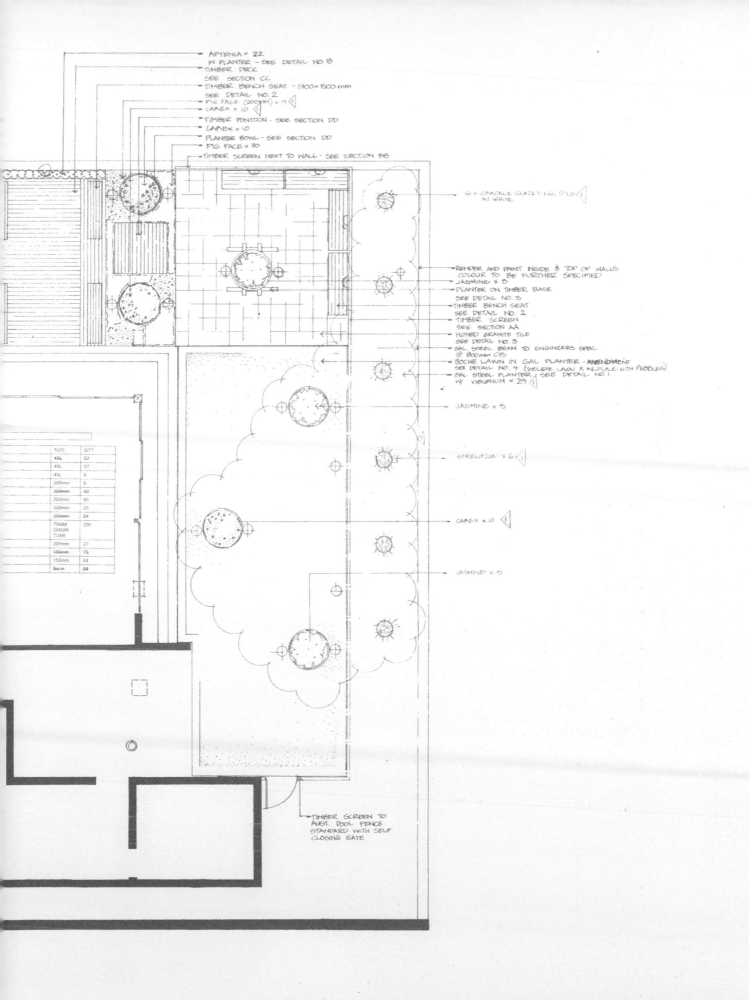

APTENIA × 22
IN PLANTER - SEE DETAIL NO. 8
TIMBER DECK
SEE SECTION CC
TIMBER BENCH SEAT - 1700×600 mm
SEE DETAIL NO. 2
PIG FACE (200mm) × 9
CAREX × 10
TIMBER PONTOON - SEE SECTION DD
CAREX × 10
PLANTER BOWL - SEE SECTION DD
PIG FACE × 70
TIMBER SCREEN NEXT TO WALL - SEE SECTION BB

6 × CRACKLE GLAZE POTS 5415
IN WHITE

RENDER AND PAINT INSIDE & TOP OF WALLS
COLOUR TO BE FURTHER SPECIFIED
JASMINE × 8
PLANTER ON TIMBER BASE
SEE DETAIL NO. 5
TIMBER BENCH SEAT
SEE DETAIL NO. 2
TIMBER SCREEN
SEE SECTION AA
HONED GRANITE TILE
SEE DETAIL NO. 3
GAL. STEEL BEAM TO ENGINEERS SPEC
@ 800mm CTS
BOCHE LAWN IN GAL PLANTER - AMENDMENT
SEE DETAIL NO. 4 (DELETE LAWN & REPLACE WITH PEBBLES)
GAL STEEL PLANTER - SEE DETAIL NO. 1
W/ VIBURNUM × 29

JASMINE × 5

STRELITZIA × 6

CAREX × 10

JASMINE × 5

SIZE	QTY
45L	57
45L	57
45L	6
300mm	6
300mm	40
200mm	90
300mm	20
300mm	24
75MM GROW TUBE	230
200mm	27
450mm	76
150mm	44
Sq.m	58

TIMBER SCREEN TO
AUST. POOL FENCE
STANDARD WITH SELF
CLOSING GATE

EDGY BUSINESS

When you start to draw up your lighting plan, it's important to consider the boundaries and access areas. Lighting the border of the space is necessary for security and for visual impact. Boundaries give the garden a sense of depth and scale. They provide standout features with a backdrop or emphasise their prominent position in the garden. A well-lit 'line' with darkness beyond creates a sense of intrigue and mystery – what's beyond the edge? – and the garden as a whole instantly gains a feeling of being enclosed within a shimmering frame.

For access areas like a driveway or a pedestrian entrance, bollards are a good choice. When you position the lights on the perimeters, it's the spacings that make all the difference. Of course, much depends on the surrounding light situation (ie street lamps or spillage from nearby buildings), but your best bet is to space them anywhere between 1200mm and 2200mm apart. The rule here is, the darker the area, the shorter the intervals, and remember to clearly accent when the path turns or changes level. Don't make the mistake of placing up-lights in a position that will shine directly into the eyes. You'll notice that most bollard lights are placed so that they shine down onto the path for this very reason.

Finally, entrance ways should always be a focus: a sort of 'announcement' of your property and a clear signpost so that it can be

ECO TIP

Solar-powered garden lights with their own solar panels require no electrical connections. Available from hardware stores and some nurseries, they are relatively expensive to buy but have no ongoing costs and cast a warm, clean light.

ILLUMINATING THE WATER *that surrounds this courtyard accentuates the feeling that the floor itself is floating (left).* FROSTED GLASS *(centre) is an excellent material for reflecting and dispersing light. Add water to the equation for tremendous visual energy and drama.* BLENDING WITH THE *furniture theme, this bollard (right) has a chunky timber base and a cap of translucent resin that disperses an even glow.*

THE OVERWHELMING HEAT and dryness of Las Vegas is legendary, and these days many outdoor cafes in the desert city compensate with misting systems which shower a fine transparent rain on the patrons, cooling and re-hydrating them. This was the inspiration behind the rainforest seen here. It is canopied with a grid of creeper-clad hoses that spray a fine mist to constantly moisten and humidify the atmosphere. Flowing sheer fabric curtains envelope the space, shutting out the world from this tropical haven. And just like dry ice creeping across a stage, clouds of vapour look fantastic backlit by the setting sun.

easily found by first-time visitors. Maybe this is where you lash out and buy that special pair of lights you've been eyeing off so that the first sight of your home makes a bold statement about what lies within.

AC/DC

There are lots of choices out there, but I find that low-voltage lights are effective in most situations. You may pay a little more to start with but the effect is well worth it and you can feel good about the fact that they are safer than most other forms of lighting. You can easily lay a 12-volt cable yourself as long as you strictly follow the advice of the manufacturer or tradesman. Anything that involves 240 volts requires a professional to do the work.

On a personal level, I love the subtlety and versatility of fibre-optic lights but,

unfortunately, it's an expensive option (isn't that always the way?) and must be installed by a licensed tradesman. Fibre optics has been around for quite some time but only in recent years have its capabilities finally begun to be exploited in the garden. It comes in the form of a thin cable (like a garden hose) filled with thin translucent strands through which the light travels and is available in a variety of different sizes. The light moves through the fibres which can bend around corners, shoot a light from the cable end or emit a soft glow through the side of the cable for its entire length. One of the best things about it is you never have to change the lights in the cable and the only maintenance required is at the box where the light originates. Fibre-optic lights can withstand all sorts of weather conditions and they're famous for illuminating difficult areas like step treads and pool surrounds.